T0320016

Fair Principles for Sustainable Development

NEW HORIZONS IN ENVIRONMENTAL ECONOMICS

General Editor: *Wallace E. Oates, Professor of Economics, University of Maryland*

This important new series is designed to make a significant contribution to the development of the principles and practices of environmental economics. It will include both theoretical and empirical work. International in scope, it will address issues of current and future concern in both East and West and in developed and developing countries.

The main purpose of the series is to create a forum for the publication of high quality work and to show how economic analysis can make a contribution to understanding and resolving the environmental problems confronting the world in the late 20th century.

Innovation in Environmental Policy
Edited by T.H. Tietenberg
Enviromental Economics
Policies for Enviromental Management and Sustainable Development
Clem Tisdell
The Economics of Solid Waste Reduction
The Impact of User Fees
Robin R. Jenkins
Fair Principles for Sustainable Development
Essays on Environmental Policy and Developing Countries
Edited by Edward Dommen

Fair Principles for Sustainable Development

Essays on Environmental Policy and Developing Countries

Edited by
Edward Dommen

United Nations Conference
on Trade and Development
Geneva, Switzerland

Published for and on behalf of the United Nations by

Edward Elgar

Published by
Edward Elgar Publishing Limited
The Lypiatts
15 Lansdown Road
Cheltenham
Glos GL50 2JA
UK

Edward Elgar Publishing, Inc.
William Pratt House
9 Dewey Court
Northampton
Massachusetts 01060
USA

This book has been printed on demand to keep the title in print.

A catalogue record for this book
is available from the British Library

Library of Congress Cataloguing in Publication Data
Fair principles for sustainable development: essays on environmental
  policy and developing countries / edited by Edward Dommen
      p. cm.
  Includes bibliographical references and index.
  1. Sustainable development—Developing countries.
2. Environmental policy—Developing countries. 3. Developing
countries—Economic policy—Environmental aspects. I. Dommen,
Edward.
HC59. 72.E5F35 1993
338.9—dc20   93–22660
                                                         CIP

ISBN 978 1 85278 912 1

Dedicated to the memory of
Frances Barron
who did so much for environmental research and negotiations

CONTENTS

CONTRIBUTORS

Gonzalo Biggs	Attorney, Senior Counsel, Inter-American Development Bank; Adjunct Professor of International Economic Relations, School of International Service, American University, Washington D.C.
Holger Bonus	Professor of Economics; Executive Director Institute for Cooperative Systems, University of Munster
Michael Bothe	Professor, Institute for Public Law, Johann-Wolfgang Goethe University, University of Frankfurt am Main
Anthony H.Chisholm	Professor and Head of Agricultural Economics and Business Management, School of Agriculture, La Trobe University, Melbourne
Harry R. Clarke	Reader in Economic School of Economics and Commerce, La Trobe University, Melbourne
Edward Dommen	Senior Economic Affairs Officer United Nations Conference on Trade and Development, Geneva
Geoffrey Heal	Professor and Vice Dean, Columbia University Graduate Business School, New York
Ferenc Juhasz	Environmental Consultant formerly with OECD
Kirit S. Parikh	Director, Indira Gandhi Institute of Development Research, Bombay

Preface
by the UNCTAD secretariat

The principles of environmental policy which are the subject of this volume have been taking root in the developed countries, but their developmental implications have still hardly been explored. It has been the task of the United Nations Conference on Trade and Development (UNCTAD) since it was founded in 1964 to insist on the developmental aspects of world economic issues, to help developing countries to share more fully in the prosperity of the world economy. This now involves exploring the relationships not just between trade and development, but between both of them and the environment. The United Nations Conference on Environment and Development, which took place in Rio de Janeiro in June 1992, explicitly invited UNCTAD to focus on the development-environment-trade triangle as a way of looking at sustainable development. UNCTAD has been asked to ensure that sustainable development is adequately reflected in its analytical work, and that this work contributes to the elaboration of innovative thinking and increased awareness in the area of environmental development economics. The present collection of essays was undertaken in this spirit.

Because of the academic character and quality of these essays, UNCTAD has chosen to publish them commercially in order to make them readily available to the community of researchers and teachers. It is pursuing work on the principles of environmental policy so as to be able to offer more direct support to intergovernmental debate and negotiations on trade, environment and development as well.

The UNCTAD secretariat is grateful to the Government of the Netherlands for its financial support which has made this project possible.

INTRODUCTION

Edward Dommen

FOUR PRINCIPLES FOR ENVIRONMENTAL POLICY

With the increasingly evident and widespread impact of economic activity on
the environment, there is a growing concern in all parts of the world that
environmental considerations should be more fully reflected in economic
decisions. Three principles are being used more and more often as guidelines
for this purpose: the Polluter-Pays Principle (PPP), the User-Pays Principle
(UPP), and the Precautionary Principle (PP). A fourth, the Subsidiarity
Principle (SP), offers guidance on the application of the first three although it
is not specifically, or even primarily, designed for environmental policy.
Originally elaborated in developed countries for their own use, these four
principles are likely to be extended to developing countries. References to
them can be found in particular in the Rio Declaration (1992)[1] adopted at the
United Nations Conference on Environment and Development (UNCED) in
June 1992. Since they appear in this statement of basic principles of environment
and development, they are all the more likely to count as factors in international
environmental negotiations in years to come.

The Polluter-Pays Principle

This principle (PPP) is the best established of the three. It was adopted by
OECD in 1972 as a fundamental principle for allocating costs of pollution
prevention and control measures introduced by the public authorities in
Member countries (OECD, 1992).[2] Since then the allocation has evolved from
partial towards full internalization of externalities. Its purpose is to induce the
polluter to bear the expenses of preventing and controlling pollution to ensure
that the environment is in an acceptable state. In other words, the cost of these
measures should be reflected in the cost of goods and services. Authoritative
texts stating and explaining the principle appear in Annex 1. Since adopting
PPP in 1972, the OECD has given considerable thought to its application and
implications, even if the actual record of its use in Member countries is uneven
(see OECD, 1989, especially Chap 2.4).

Principle 16 of the Rio Declaration highlights the essential features of PPP:

National authorities should endeavour to promote the internalization of environmental costs and the use of economic instruments, taking into account the approach that the polluter should, in principle, bear the cost of pollution, with due regard to the public interest and without distorting international trade in investment.

The drafters intended that text to cover the UPP as well as PPP. The reference to promoting the use of economic instruments is perhaps particularly relevant with respect to UPP.

The User-Pays Principle

The basic idea of PPP is embraced in the broader UPP, which is concerned with resource pricing rather than pollution. Indeed, the OECD tends to refer to it simply as resource pricing, treating it more as a question of common sense than as a principle.[3] It has not been elaborated to the same degree as PPP. Indeed, there is not enough agreement on the definition of UPP for it to have been officially adopted by the OECD.[4] In Annex 2 an informal note is reproduced which describes UPP. It emanated from the OECD in 1988.

Essentially, UPP states that the price of a natural resource should reflect the full range of the costs involved in using it, including the costs of the external effects associated with exploiting, transforming and using the resource, together with the costs of future uses foregone.

The Precautionary Principle

This principle (PP) was first officially mentioned in the Ministerial Declaration of the Second International Conference on the Protection of the North Sea (1987) and fully stated in the Bergen Ministerial Declaration of May 1990 (Cameron and Werksman, 1991). Paragraph 7 reads:

In order to achieve sustainable development, policies must be based on the Precautionary Principle. Environmental measures must anticipate, prevent and attack the causes of environmental degradation. Where there are threats of serious or irreversible damage, lack of full scientific certainty should not be used as a reason for postponing measures to prevent environmental degradation.[5]

PP has rapidly been integrated into official thinking in developed countries. For instance, it was reaffirmed by the OECD Environment Committee meeting at ministerial level in January 1991.[6] Notwithstanding such ministerial endorsement, the principle remains controversial in international negotiations. It is therefore remarkable that Principle 15 of the Rio Declaration closely follows the text quoted above, the main difference being that the Precautionary Principle is demoted to a 'precautionary approach':

In order to protect the environment, the precautionary approach shall be widely applied by States according to their capabilities. Where there are threats of serious or irreversible damage, lack of full scientific certainty shall not be used as a reason for postponing cost-effective measures to prevent environmental degradation.

National policy decisions which involve threats of serious or irreversible damage are still taken in many cases, even in developed countries, with little regard for this principle.

The Subsidiarity Principle

The essence of this principle (SP) is that political decisions should be taken at the lowest possible level. Well rooted in constitutional practice in countries like Switzerland, it has been absorbed into the practice of the European Community. It is reflected in the Single European Act in the subsection dealing with the environment (Article 130R.4): 'The Community shall take action relating to the environment to the extent to which the objectives ... can be attained better at the Community level than at the level of the individual Member states' The Treaty on European Union ('Treaty of Maastricht') expresses the spirit of subsidiarity in its first lines, which talk of 'decisions taken as closely as possible to the citizen'.[7] Article 3b is even more explicit:

> In areas which do not fall within its exclusive competence, the Community shall take action, in accordance with the principle of subsidiarity, only if and in so far as the objectives of the proposed action cannot be sufficiently achieved by the Member States and can therefore, by reason of the scale or effects of the proposed action, be better achieved by the Community.

It is also reflected in Article 4 of the Council of Europe's European Charter of local self–government:

> ... Local authorities shall, within the limits of the law, have full discretion to exercise their initiative with regard to any matter which is not excluded from their competence nor assigned to any other authority. ...

> Public responsibility shall generally be exercised, in preference, by those authorities which are closest to the citizen. Allocation of responsibility to another authority should weigh up the extent and nature of the task and requirements of efficiency and economy.

A reference to SP can be discerned in Principle 10 of the Rio Declaration, which states that 'environmental issues are best handled with the participation of all concerned citizens, at the relevant level.' It is also applied conversely in Principle 12, which states that 'Environmental measures addressing transboundary or global environmental problems should, as far as possible, be based on an international consensus.'

Application of SP is quite likely to result in different collectivities taking different decisions on similar problems. PPP recognizes explicitly that this is likely to happen: 'differing national environmental policies ... are justified by a variety of factors including ... different social objectives and priorities attached to environmental protection'.[8]

SP simply reflects normal management practice nowadays. More fundamentally, it requires popular participation; it aims to ensure that local interests are articulated and incorporated into the decision-making process. In this regard, Jacques Delors, President of the European Commission, stated in a speech in March 1991 'Subsidiarity arises from a moral demand which makes respect for the dignity and responsibility of the people who compose it the objective of every society ... it is also an obligation for superior authority to act regarding that person or that collectivity so as to give them the means of their fulfillment.'[9]

PPP requires political decisions. Its basic objective is that the environment be in an acceptable state.[10] The more recent OECD recommendation on the application of PPP to accidental pollution emphasizes that polluters should meet the cost of reasonable measures to prevent and control accidental pollution.[11] PP comes into play when 'there are threats of serious or irreversible damage'. 'Acceptable', 'reasonable' and 'serious' are political notions. They can be rendered operational only by a decision which is political in nature. SP urges that these decisions be taken by the authorities which are closest to the populations concerned. UPP can also work only on the basis of decisions which are political in nature, if only to settle which non-use resource values to include in estimating total economic value (see Figure 1.1 and the corresponding text in Chapter 1). As Chisholm and Clarke imply, PP can also call SP into action, at least in deciding whether administrative costs are excessive or not. SP can also be a sensible policy where risk is concerned, e.g. in reaching a political decision with regard to subjective probabilities or 'evidentiary thresholds' (Chisholm and Clarke, Chap. 7).

Strictly taken, SP concerns the geographical level at which political decisions should be taken, even though the European Charter of local self government leaves the door open to other interpretations when it refers to 'those authorities which are closest to the citizen'. A geographical criterion can be sensible in many cases but inappropriate in others. SP can in certain circumstances help guide the application of the basic environmental principles which are the main subject of this volume, but its role in this context is only subsidiary.

Environment and Sustainable Development

The foregoing principles have been elaborated in the developed world primarily for use there. The purpose of this volume is to look at environmental policy instruments from a developmental perspective. Its starting point is more precisely the concept of sustainable development, defined by the World

Commission on Environment and Development in 1987 (WCED, 1987) as follows:

> Sustainable development is development that meets the needs of the present without compromising the ability of future generations to meet their own needs. It contains within it two key concepts:
>
> the concept of 'needs', in particular the essential needs of the world's poor, to which overriding priority should be given; and
>
> the idea of limitations imposed by the state of technology and social organization on the environment's ability to meet present and future needs.

This definition was welcomed by the United Nations General Assembly, which recorded 'the imperative need for making the transition towards sustainable development' (General Assembly resolution 42/187, paras.1 and 2).

The principles with which this study is concerned have by and large only recently been formulated. There is still little experience with their use even in developed economies. Although PPP is 20 years old, its record of application remains thin although it is now being applied more systematically and energetically in OECD countries. Little thought has been given to what would happen if the principles were applied within developing countries or to their international trade. The purpose of these essays is to encourage reflection on this question and above all to stimulate it. Indeed, to examine the principles from a developmental perspective can be revealing in more ways than one. Ferenc Juhasz, who has worked on PPP and UPP for many years in the OECD secretariat, said that in writing his essay he discovered completely new ideas concerning the implementation of PPP.

Five of the authors in this collection were asked to examine the concept of PPP along with UPP in a broad perspective and to comment on the merits, drawbacks and technical feasibility for developing countries of applying these principles. For this reason, these five authors were chosen from a variety of disciplines and backgrounds (see 'About the authors'). Anthony Chisholm and Harry Clarke (Chap. 7) were asked to examine the Precautionary Principle, and Michael Bothe to explore the contribution the Subsidiarity Principle could make to the three environmental principles.

As was to be expected, nay hoped, with respect to this novel question, the answers are diverse: each sheds a different light on the issue. In Chapter 1, the editor has attempted to single out the points the authors have raised which are especially important for development policy, and to offer further comments and argument to support an application of the principles which would serve the development, the sustainable development, of developing countries.

NOTES

1 Rio Declaration on Environment and Development A/CONF.151/26,1992
2 OECD (1992b) contains these and further statements.
3 Viz. e.g. 'Water resource management: integration, demand management, and groundwater protection', Recommendation C(89)12 (Final) adopted on 31 March 1989; quoted in OECD (1992b).
4 See F. Juhasz, Chap. 2, Application of the OECD principles, A(ii)e, p. 21.
5 The Declaration was adopted at the Regional Conference on the follow-up to the report of the World Commission on Environment and Development in the ECE Region, held in Bergen, Norway on 8–16 May 1990.
6 OECD Environment Committee at Ministerial Level, Communiqué, Paris, 31 January 1991, para. 38.
7 Treaty on European Union, Title I, Article A.
8 Annex 1,'Guiding principles', para. 6. Annex 1 presents a number of OECD recommendations and supporting texts concerning PPP. The notes in this volume refer to them by abbreviations of their titles.
9 Quoted in Domaine public, Lausanne, 2 May 1991.
10 Annex 1, e.g. 'Guiding principles', para. 3.
11 OECD (1992), 'The application of the Polluter-Pays Principle to accidental pollution' (Recommendation adopted on 7 July 1989), Appendix, para.4.

1. THE FOUR PRINCIPLES FOR ENVIRONMENTAL POLICY AND SUSTAINABLE DEVELOPMENT: AN OVERVIEW

Edward Dommen

The purpose of this volume of essays is to explore what the implications would be for developing countries if the four principles – Polluter-Pays, User-Pays, Precautionary and Subsidiarity Principles – were more widely applied, in particular in international trade and global environmental agreements. This chapter focuses on the implications for two types of entity. Firstly, it attempts to discern situations in which the principles have effects on developing countries as countries in the world economy as distinct from the effects on developed countries. Secondly, it focuses on the impact the principles could have on those people to whose essential needs sustainable development assigns overriding priority: the world's poor.[1]

It makes the simplifying assumption that the world's poor are located in developing countries; in so far as they are in developed countries, the policy remedies remain much the same, but their implementation becomes a matter for the developed countries themselves rather than for North–South relations.

This chapter attempts to point out lines of policy analysis which can be used in North–South deliberations on development or the environment. It attempts to stress the lines of more immediate negotiating interest contained in the other essays in this volume and to bring them together in a systematic way. On the other hand, it does not attempt to present a complete taxonomy of situations. Rather, it singles out particular cases and implies that the other cases of the same class can be worked out if necessary: if readers notice asymmetries in the presentation, like a discussion of demand curves not matched by a corresponding discussion of supply curves, or a reference to developing countries but not to the poor, they should take it as a signal that the missing aspects can be developed in a similar manner.

This chapter is articulated first around the Polluter-Pays Principle (PPP) and then the User-Pays Principle (UPP). Their application involves the economic problem of uncertainty. When that occurs, the Precautionary Principle (PP) is brought in as a supporting element. Both the main principles and the Precautionary Principle involve questions of political priorities and popular perceptions. Political decisions are therefore inescapable. While the Subsidiarity Principle (SP) is far from able to provide guidelines for the location of all political decisions, it has a valuable contribution to make in many respects. These guidelines are discussed at appropriate points in the argument below. The chapter ends with a discussion of the relative roles of market and other mechanisms in using the four principles to achieve sustainable development.

A single fundamental idea underlies the principles which are the subject of this volume: those who benefit from an activity should meet the full range of the costs it generates. The spontaneous working of the free market will not meet this objective if externalities, collective goods or uncertainty are involved. Resource depletion and irreversible changes to the environment which constrain the freedom of future generations to meet their own needs can also fall prey to market failures. The three environmental principles provide a standard framework within which these failures can be remedied. PPP and UPP are designed to deal with a wide range of them. PP responds to one only: uncertainty. An extremely summary but not incorrect statement in the context of environmental policy would be that SP deals specifically with information. It not only implies that the people who have information to offer should be involved in decision-making, but it also recognizes the need to respect subjective views of reality if policies are to be politically acceptable.

The advantage of standard cost allocation and policy guidelines is not only that they save time and energy for hard-pressed policy-makers but that they also 'encourage the rational use and the better allocation of scarce environmental resources and prevent the appearance of distortions in international trade and investment'.[2]

THE POLLUTER-PAYS PRINCIPLE

Who Actually Pays?

With respect to PPP, OECD states that the costs of pollution prevention and control measures should be reflected in the cost of goods and services which cause pollution.[3] UPP, which is supposed to include PPP, states that the price for the use of a resource should be the full long-run marginal social cost of using it, including the external costs associated with its development and any resultant pollution prevention and control activities. In such a system the price reflects the environmental costs to the community of satisfying the marginal demand.[4]

It is stated in Annex 1 that: 'From the point of view of conformity with the Polluter-Pays Principle, it does not matter whether the polluter passes on to his prices some or all of the environment costs or absorbs them'.[5] However, from the point of view of developing countries, or more generally of the distribution of opportunities and income between rich and poor, it can matter a great deal. The degree to which the costs internalized by PPP and UPP are paid by either the consumer or the producer depends to a large extent on the elasticity of the supply and demand curves. Given the supply curve, the more inelastic the demand curve, the greater the share of externalities internalized which will be borne by consumers. Conversely, given the demand curve, the more inelastic the supply curve the greater the share which will be borne by producers. The costs will be borne entirely by consumers only if the supply curve is horizontal. If the demand curve is horizontal, the costs will be borne entirely by producers.

Many of the goods and indeed services exported by developing countries are relatively undifferentiated. The demand curve facing any given exporter is therefore likely to be elastic. The supply curve, on the other hand, is likely to be fairly inelastic given on the one hand the urgent need for foreign exchange and on the other the conditions under which exports are produced. In short, given the shape of supply and demand curves, PPP applied to the exports of developing countries is likely to impose a burden mainly on the producing country in so far as prices are determined by arms-length transactions in the market. However, a significant part of world commodity trade takes the form of intra-firm transactions at transfer prices designed to concentrate profits in the place which suits the firm best. This is often not the commodity exporting country. In such circumstances, the costs internalized through PPP might well be internalized elsewhere without adversely affecting at least the price received by the producing country.

In addition to the situation just mentioned, certain categories of poor people in developing countries face conditions similar to those described above. In so far as they depend on the market to provide what they need, their demand curve is likely to be very inelastic: the poor have no more than enough to meet their essential needs and these needs are urgent.[6] Whatever the shape of their demand curve, the urban poor in any event have little to offer on the market other than their labour. They will offer as much labour as is physically possible since, whatever its price, it will not cover their needs in many cases (Lipton, 1983). The supply curve for such an individual's labour is very inelastic. Meanwhile, employers face an abundance of candidates. For both these reasons, any increased costs will be borne not so much by the rich but by the poor to the extent that they depend on the market.[7]

Whether it is the producer or the consumer who actually pays under the Polluter-Pays Principle depends not only on the shape of the supply and demand curves, but also on the ability of the parties to shift the curves. Environmental concerns can lead to a shift in the demand curve, for example, the declining demand for fur goods in developed countries. One way in which the growing environmental consciousness of the consuming public in developed countries expresses itself is through a heightened perception of the non-use values of resources (Figure 1.1). To the degree that the price of a resource explicitly incorporates these considerations, the demand curve for the resource may shift outwards. When firms use ecological arguments in their advertising, they presumably expect demand curves to shift as a result.

One of the avowed purposes of PPP is to encourage producers to develop new, cleaner technologies, which may actually be more profitable than the technologies they replace. This is certainly the case with respect to 'no regrets' technologies. How these profits are distributed remains an issue in sustainable development. New technologies are normally private intellectual property, while the technology they replace may be in the public domain. The result may be an increased flow of income to developed countries, i.e. to the firms located there which own the patents. If the new technology is imposed through inappropriate forms of international environmental standards, the net result may even be on balance unfavourable to developing countries or *mutatis mutandis* to small enterprises run by the poor.

The actual allocation of costs and benefits between producers and consumers as a result of a shift in supply and demand curves depends on the type of case. The important point is that the power to shift either curve is concentrated. Power over supply curves rests for instance with firms which have the means to invest in the development of new technology or with institutions including governments disposing of funds to support this kind of research. Power over the demand curve rests largely in the first instance with the media and therefore more fundamentally with those who have access to them. These include not only economic enterprises, but also well-organized lobbies, including environmental ones. All these forms of power tend to be located preponderantly in the developed countries. Since it is normal for any power to be exercised in the interests of those who yield it, there is no reason for it to serve the needs of the target groups of sustainable development – the poor and future generations – except where these fortuitously coincide with the interests of the powerful. This having been said, it is certainly useful to explore the effects of shifts in supply and demand curves in each particular case so that such serendipity can be exploited whenever possible.

It is generally accepted that the poor are more risk-averse than the rich. They lack the wealth with which to cushion losses or increased costs resulting from unfavourable outcomes. They tend therefore to choose strategies which exclude negative outcomes. They are in short inclined to observe the Precautionary Principle. The question of risk aversion takes on wider and even global scope when the world's rich choose strategies which contain negative outcomes, the cost of which falls on the poor, not to mention future generations. The world's poor have more to gain than the rich from including the Precautionary Principle in international agreements.

Setting Standards

PPP determines a set of measures to ensure that the environment is in an acceptable state. What counts as an acceptable state is decided by public authorities through a process of collective choice.[8]

At the international level it is repeatedly insisted that each country is free to set its own standards. Thus the Statement by the UNEP Governing Council on sustainable development says 'Sustainable development ... does not imply in any way encroachment upon national sovereignty'.[9] That this is likely to result in different standards being set in different countries is perfectly understandable. Firstly, a crucial criterion for judging the economic efficiency of sustainable natural resource use is the equation of real marginal costs and benefits including environmental protection and resource conservation. If different countries all adopt PPP and UPP to this end, environmental standards may well differ as a result of differences in resource endowment and cost functions. The OECD states the argument plainly: 'Differing national environmental policies ... are justified by a variety of factors including ... different pollution assimilative capacities of the environment in its present state, different social objectives and priorities attached to environmental protection and different degrees of industrialization and population density'.[10]

Societies may have different priorities as well as different resource endowments. It is especially plausible to argue that if the average citizen is convinced of the need to devote more material and human resources to achieve a better environment as his or her income rises, communities with higher incomes will assign a higher priority to the environment (Baumol and Oates 1988, Chap. 15; GATT, 1992). These differences serve the dynamic interests of sustainable development in that firstly they facilitate economic growth and secondly sustainable development requires economic growth in places where the essential needs of the world's poor are not being met (WCED, 1987, p.44). The end result is that once the communities become richer, they will themselves share the view of the already rich that the environment deserves a higher priority.

Although states have the sovereign right to set their own environmental standards, multilateral cooperation is often indispensable. One of the main purposes of PPP is indeed to avoid distortions in international trade and investment. If all countries agree on the principles not only by which prices are determined but also by which certain processes or products are disallowed, in

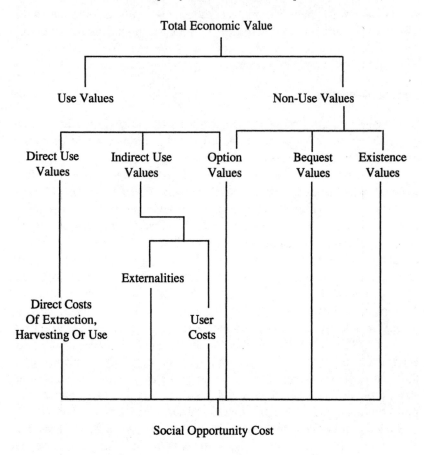

Figure 1.1   Resource Value and Cost *

* *This figure and the text describing it are based on UNCTAD (1991)*

particular PPP, UPP and PP, free trade will induce shifts in production, leading to a more efficient and sustainable use of environmental resources throughout the world.

Thus even when pollution or resource depletion are purely internal to a given state, the efficiency of international trade invites agreement on the rules by which economic decisions are taken. Avoiding trade distortion may well justify setting limits to the types of policy mechanism which may be used. It is in this spirit that PPP takes such a strong position against subsidies.

Environmental Costs

PPP is pragmatic. It 'is no more than an efficiency principle for allocating costs and does not involve bringing pollution down to an optimum level of any type, although it does not exclude the possibility of doing so'.[11] Even if the authorities are not trying to determine a pollution charge which is optimum in a strict sense, they still need to have an idea of both abatement and damage costs.

Abatement costs are difficult to estimate not only in developing, but also in developed countries. The difficulties spring from the complexity of relations between levels of production and output of pollutants, which may be non-linear or even the result of physical or chemical interaction between different pollutants emitted by different processes and in different places. They also spring from human factors which may be difficult to cost, like inculcating a sense of responsibility in staff who operate hazardous processes. Estimating damage costs can also be problematic even in developed countries, especially when the damage is dispersed over a large number of people who cannot easily make their losses known. It may be difficult to assign a monetary value to damage caused by insidious processes like noise. Some new product or processes may cause damage which becomes apparent only many years later. Several carcinogens, not to mention chlorofluorocarbons, are examples. They should presumably fall under the Precautionary Principle; they cannot otherwise be internalized through PPP.

Collective Choice

Ronald Coase (1960) in his famous article 'The Problem of Social Cost' assumes that a fully articulated economy is composed of mobile factors of production. This is an idealization even with respect to developed economies. It can be far from the reality of developing countries where economies are not fully articulated, so that the range of choices assumed by Coase is not fully available. The very notion of comparing values becomes dubious in societies in which some sections of the population depend on non-monetary activity to meet a share of their essential needs, or in societies in which various cultures with different relationships to the monetary economy live side by side. Even in homogeneous highly-monetized societies, efficiency considerations, let alone equity ones, would encourage a preference for methods of collective choice which offer direct involvement to the parties concerned. They have more information about actual abatement and damage costs than can be distilled to higher levels of decision. Given the complexity of relationships, which can lead to different outcomes in different places, and the difficulty if not impossibility of representing the costs by predictable mathematical functions, efficiency calls for gathering as much factual information as possible. When PPP talks of decision by public authorities 'through a collective choice and with respect to the limited information available'[12] it must surely imply a participatory political process, because it is indispensable both to bringing a fuller range of costs to light and to generating a preference ranking between outcomes.

Given furthermore that money may be a misleading and in some cases incomprehensible yardstick, even the quest for Pareto optimality requires the use of qualitative measures as well as quantitative economic signals. A Pareto optimum is a position where no one can become better off without someone becoming worse off. It has achieved eminence in economic theory because it avoids the need to make interpersonal comparisons of utility; economists are well aware that such comparisons are subject to grave pitfalls. Since the Pareto optimum eschews interpersonal comparisons, it can rest only on self-evaluation. It is for each person to assess whether or not he or she is better off in one position than in another. In cases where the market does not reveal the answer, other methods must be used. Where the economy is segmented or non-monetary activities are important to some parties, determining Pareto optima can only pass through processes of consultation, i.e. political processes.

Some environmental issues have direct international effects in that activities in one country give rise to environmental externalities in others. It is necessary to insist that in such cases the corresponding policy decision should be taken by all the parties concerned: there have been a number of cases in recent years in which one or a few developed countries have taken steps to impose their own standards on other countries. Regardless of whether the spillover effects are physical or merely psychological, the policy recommendation remains the same.[13] To reach agreement bilaterally or multilaterally is an expression of respect for national sovereignty. Solutions achieved in this way are likely to be not only more equitable, but also more efficient because they consider a wider range of conditions and use more information to find the solution (GATT, 1992). In such cases, the Subsidiarity Principle calls for decisions to be taken at a level embracing a number of countries.

The Polluters, the Victims and the Others

If it is accepted that all parties affected should have a say in setting the environmental standards around which PPP revolves, a new problem arises. The world does not divide into the three categories of polluters, victims and unaffected. The degree to which and the way in which externalities are internalized have effects which go beyond the polluters and the victims. They can for instance have macroeconomic effects, in particular on employment throughout the economy or in particular regions. This is recognized in the

Recommendation of the OECD Council on the Implementation of the Polluter-Pays Principle.[14]

The economy at large is affected through the dynamic effects of these policy decisions as well, and in particular the impetus they give to technological innovation. Governments are willing to accept static inefficiencies in order to capture dynamic advantage. One of the arguments in favour of the Basel Convention on the Control of Transboundary Movements of Hazardous Wastes and their Disposal was precisely that it could stimulate methods of production which generated fewer hazardous wastes and that there could be competitive advantage in pressing innovation in that direction.[15] The existence of parties other than the polluters and their victims provides a possibility for the two to act together. They need not simply struggle to shift the burden of environmental costs among themselves, they can league together to pass them on to other parts of society. In a short-term or narrow perspective, this can be an attractive technique. Environmental protectionism provides examples. The producers of pollution and their victims jointly agree to abatement measures which raise costs. In order to protect the producers' market, these measures are accompanied by protectionist ones to prevent competition from imports pressing the producers to absorb the costs or to think of new technologies to deal with the original problem. The environmental costs are thus shifted to the domestic consumers of the product in question and to the potential producers abroad.

Subsidies

Another technique is to resort to subsidies, in other words to draw on public revenue to get both the polluters and their victims off the hook. PPP strictly circumscribes this device. The OECD loses no opportunity to emphasize that PPP excludes subsidies except in a clearly specified set of cases. Juhasz summarizes the arguments against subsidies. Furthermore, it can be formally established that under pure competition, although a subsidy will tend to reduce the emissions of the firm, it is apt to increase the emissions of the industry beyond what they would be in the absence of the subsidy (Baumol and Oates, 1988, Chap. 14). In essence, while the subsidy encourages cleaner methods or products, it reduces their price below what they would be without the subsidy; this in turn increases the quantity demanded, thereby increasing total pollution even though pollution per unit has been reduced. In other words subsidies may well worsen the environmental problem they were intended to alleviate.

PPP recognizes that subsidies may be provided when the application of PPP without subsidies would 'jeopardize the social and economic policy objectives of a country or region. This would be the case for example, when the additional expenditure incurred by polluting industries would result in holding back regional development or adversely affecting the labour market'.[16] A subsidy, tax advantage or other similar measure should however be strictly limited, And in particular comply with every one of the following conditions:

(a) It should be selective and restricted to those parts of the economy, such as industries, areas or plants, where severe difficulties would otherwise occur;
(b) It should be limited to well-defined transitional periods, laid down in advance and adapted to the specific socio-economic problems associated with the implementation of a country's environmental programme;
(c) It should not create significant distortions in international trade and investment.[17]

The severe difficulties described in provision (a) above are often encountered in developing countries. Their economies are often less fully articulated than those of developed countries, and so a smooth adjustment to new requirements is difficult. To impose additional costs on polluters can threaten employment or the viability of sectors important to much of the national economy. However, subsidies impose the burden of costs on the taxpayer rather than on the polluter or consumer and may even increase the total burden of environmental costs on society as a whole. In developing countries taxpayers may be poor and furthermore government revenue derives mainly from indirect taxes. In so far as the cost of pollution or pollution avoidance is imposed on poor communities, when it could be borne by the polluter or by the consumer of the goods or services the polluter produces, the overriding principle of sustainable development is violated.

Furthermore, where income is low, response to income incentives is likely to be high. This concerns not only the polluter, but also the taxpayers. Reducing taxpayers' disposable income in order to subsidize a polluter is likely to have a disincentive effect throughout the economy. Thus, in developing countries, subsidies are likely to be both statically and dynamically inefficient. The two foregoing paragraphs do not exhaust the analysis which should be pursued to take a policy decision in any particular case with respect to equity in income distribution. The environmental costs or externalities are present in any event. To internalize these costs through taxes or regulatory measures shifts the incidence one way; to provide subsidies shifts them another. There are three positions to be compared: with a tax, with a subsidy and with no charge.

Apart from income distribution, the OECD presumption bluntly stated is that subsidies promote inefficiency and backwardness. In so far as rigidity or lack of alternatives makes subsidies necessary in the short run, it should be possible to determine the time needed for the subsidized activity to give way to one which contributes more to the economy. Hence the importance of provision (b) of the OECD Recommendation quoted above according to which the length of the transitional period should be laid down in advance (as Samuel

Johnson said, 'When a man knows he is to be hanged in a fortnight, it concentrates his mind wonderfully' (Boswell, 1777). Although this provision provides an essential incentive to adjust, it is often neglected in developed countries.

Income Effects

The consequences for the consumer of a rise in price can be divided into an income effect and a substitution effect. To some extent, the consumer compensates for the rise in price by substituting goods which have become relatively cheaper compared with the goods whose price has risen. These substitute goods have not, however, become cheaper relative to the consumer's fixed income. The net result is that income falls. For a prosperous consumer, an increase in the price of any one good has only a slight effect on his or her income. For the poor, struggling to meet their families' essential needs, the income effect may be pronounced. For this reason as well as those having to do with the shape of supply and demand curves, the introduction of PPP and UPP is likely to fall particularly on the poor in so far as the price mechanism is chosen as the vehicle.

Furthermore, the foregoing assumes that consumers can choose a substitute, and that they have a range of choices available to them which more or less meet their needs. However, as Parikh points out in this volume, the poor may have little choice about how to meet their needs.

Subsidies should be distinguished from income support. Sustainable development recognizes that the poor need support. Ideally, this involves ensuring that they have the means to meet their own needs through their own productive work. If this is not immediately possible, basic income should be provided through mechanisms of social solidarity. When the application of PPP would, taken by itself, lead to a reduction in the living standards of the poor, e.g. by raising the price of an essential consumption good, the proper response is not to subsidize that particular economic transaction, but to provide offsetting income support. The poor can then allocate their income in the light of prices which reflect costs, including social and environmental costs, to the fullest extent possible.

Should the Victim be Paid?

A simple sense of justice suggests that if the polluter should pay,[18] then the victim should surely be paid. Efficiency arguments do not point in that direction. If victims are fully compensated for damages incurred, they have no incentive to take remedial action that is within their reach. It may be cheaper for the victim rather than the polluter to take preventive action. This is a key point in Ronald Coase's article, 'The Problem of Social Cost' (1960) (see also Baumol and Oates (1988), Chap. 3, sections 4–5).

For this type of argument to yield an equitable outcome, a degree of equality in bargaining power and in freedom of choice between the polluter and the victim must be assumed. Such equality is more likely to be lacking in a developing than in a developed country.

Let us examine the problem by dividing it into four types of case. The assumption that the poor have not only a lower income, but also fewer choices or less freedom of action than the rich underlies all the cases discussed below.

Let us first take the case in which the poor are victims of pollution generated by the rich, e.g. their air is poisoned by the effluvia from a large factory or their water by pesticides. Although the cost to the poor may be high, for instance shorter life expectancy, they may not be able to afford to move to a healthier environment. They are also likely to be uneducated or ill-informed and thus unaware of the costs or risks they are incurring. In short, imposing pollution costs on the poor may bring about little substitution; it may stimulate a constructive and innovative response on the part of the victims only to a limited degree. The effect is more likely to be confined to reducing their income, welfare or life-span and impoverishing them further. The imperative of sustainable development disapproves of activities with this kind of consequence. The aim of PPP is precisely to avoid activities which have unacceptable environmental consequences. If however an appropriate political process has determined that the measure is acceptable, then the overriding priority due to the essential needs of the poor requires that they be compensated. Economic efficiency urges that the compensation take a form which widens the poor's range of choices, so that they can use their own creativity to respond to the situation. Financial compensation is not necessarily a good solution. Better education, job creation or even measures like improved public transport so that the poor could afford to live in nicer areas but still commute easily to their jobs, might all be practical uses for pollution charges levied on relatively rich polluters.

As a second case, let us consider poor polluters whose victims are rich. The poor may cause pollution as consumers or producers. A result of PPP in a market economy will be that the cost of keeping the environment in an acceptable state will be reflected in consumer prices. We have already pointed out that if the consumers are poor, the income effects are likely to outweigh the substitution effects. Another consequence may be not to encourage environmentally sounder choice, but rather to drive the poor consumer to environmentally worse behaviour which has the advantage from their point of view of falling outside the monetary economy. Imposing a charge on rubbish collection may encourage them to dispose of their rubbish in the easiest way, which may be unsightly if not a hazard for public health. Fuel costs including an allowance for environmental effects, like global warming, would encourage the poor to resort to fuel, like charcoal or dung, obtained outside the formal economy thereby aggravating more immediate environmental damage like deforestation or failure to return organic matter to the soil (see also Parikh). In these cases, it is in the self-interest of the rich to meet pollution avoidance costs.

The poor are likely to be small producers: large enterprises require concentrations of capital which are beyond the reach of the poor. As small producers, the poor are likely to face relatively horizontal demand curves. We have seen that in such cases PPP imposes the costs of pollution control on the producer rather than on the consumer. Given the relatively few choices open to the poor, they may be compelled to save not so much on the cost of activities which spare the environment, but rather on those costs which are not immediately indispensable to reducing the output they sell, The net result may be more severe pollution. A subsidy policy in line with Annex 1 of Recommendation III.2b may provide a solution: assistance measures could be adapted to the specific socio-economic problems associated with the environmental problem and designed to raise the income-earning capacity of the polluters, so that within a well-defined transitional period they can afford to change to more environmentally sound methods or activities.

A second solution is available to the rich: rather than deal directly with the pollution, the rich may prefer to shift their burden to the poor. Crime is an example. It is a particularly common externality which the poor impose on the rich in the cities in the developing world. In the history of Western Europe, far-reaching structural policies involving *inter alia* labour–management relations, education and macroeconomic employment policies have greatly reduced personal insecurity compared with a few centuries ago. Alternatively, the apparatus of repression and exclusion can be strengthened so that the poor turn on each other rather than on the rich. While this solution may be economically efficient it countervenes the fundamental principle of sustainable development.

The third case in which the poor pollute the poor is the most intractable. PPP can hardly be enforced in a society in which the priorities of all members are dominated by their most immediate needs. Higher income is often the only way out. As the World Commission on Environment and Development says, sustainable development clearly requires economic growth in places where the essential needs of the poor are not met (WCED, 1987, p. 44). Economic growth requires capital which can only be provided by those who, being free from the demands of their immediate needs, can accumulate it. The vicious circle of environmental degradation fuelled by despair can be broken only with resources provided by the rich. Given the value of PPP for the static and dynamic efficiency of the economy, the third case underlines that when the polluters are poor and powerless, and have few choices, it is in everyone's interests to ensure that they have the means to pay.

The fourth and last case is that in which the rich pollute the rich. This is the type of situation which Coase (1960) had in mind, like most of the economists who have followed him. Both polluter and the victims enjoy freedom of choice and the economy in which they function allows smooth passage from one activity to another. The cases Coase describes actually involve bargaining between small numbers of relatively balanced interests, the outcome being a payment from polluter to victim or vice versa. If on the other hand the number of victims is large, efficient treatment prohibits compensation (Baumol and Oates, 1988, Chap. 4); however, a range of more or less acceptable choices available to both polluters and victims remains a key ethical presupposition of the argument.

All these cases assume the existence of both polluters and victims and stress those cases in which power or freedom of choice is unequally distributed between them. The distribution of power is at its most unequal when the victims do not yet exist. Sustainable development focuses on them when it states that 'sustainable development is development that meets the needs of the present without comprising the ability of future generations to meet their own needs'. PPP does not provide for this aspect of sustainable development except in so far as those who decide whether the environment is in an acceptable state include people or organizations who take upon themselves to act as judges and defenders of the needs of future generations and they may be unreliable as surrogates. UPP addresses the issue of justice between generations more directly.

POLLUTERS AND USERS

One drawback of the Polluter-Pays Principle which is not as trivial as some may think, is that the term 'polluter' has emotive undertones. Essentially pollution implies not only a physical or chemical phenomenon, but also the existence of someone who is affected by it. The words 'pollution' and 'polluter' are biased in that they convey a sense of blame against the source of the physical phenomenon. A more neutral approach would be to see the situation as one of competing demands on a given medium. Bonus in this volume cites the example of the local air mantle which can be utilized as a medium of silence or as a carrier for the disposal of noise. Competing demands for the medium give it a value, transforming it into a resource. This is an essential conceptual step which explains why PPP can be regarded as a special case of UPP.[19] It is from this standpoint that Heal focuses so directly on property rights in his chapter of this volume. If a resource has value, *inter alia,* as a medium for disposing of pollution, it is important for efficiency, equity and the encouragement of innovation to determine who has the right to appropriate the value of the resource. There are practical differences between them. According to PPP, public authorities determine measures to ensure that the environment is in an acceptable state. The polluter should bear the expenses of carrying out these measures, i.e. of refraining from polluting beyond a certain level. If the means are process or product standards, regulations or prohibitions,[20] the polluter may use the resource which the particular medium constitutes free of charge up to that level. On the other hand, PPP also includes pollution charges among its mechanisms.[21] In this case, the polluter actually pays for the resource used, which corresponds to UPP. In many ways, UPP and PPP appear to conflict and in his chapter in this volume Juhasz describes many instances of overlap. Work remains to harmonze the two.

THE USER-PAYS PRINCIPLE

UPP applies to resources in general, not only commodities traditionally traded like coffee or copper, but also environmental resources like water, air (including climate) soil or ecosystems. From this perspective, PPP underlines one aspect of the costs of using these resources: basically the externalities shown in Figure 1.1

In policy terms, however, UPP deals with a set of issues largely different from PPP: as Juhasz says; PPP is used in OECD countries for efficiency and cost effectiveness in pollution control measures, while resource pricing is used for efficient use of natural resources and for minimizing the environmental impact of the use of these resources.

The basic principle in resource pricing is that those who benefit should pay. The expectation is that adopting UPP as a basis for charging for resource use and consequently for allocating the resource would be a major factor in reducing conflicts over resource use, minimizing environmental and social impacts and improving resource use efficiency. UPP underlies an economic policy for the management of resources which ties the beneficiaries of the use of the resource to the associated costs.[22]

As Juhasz explains, the OECD originally elaborated UPP with respect to water. Although it might at first seem that water pricing is a local issue which the principle of subsidiarity would leave to local authorities, Heal explains that even the pricing of this resource can have significant consequences for international trade, and in particular for developing countries.

The following paragraphs will recapitulate three sets of issue involved in the UPP: the total value of a resource, the property rights through which it may be expressed and the identification of the user.

The Components of Resource Value

The total economic value of a resource and the corresponding social opportunity cost of its use are illustrated in Figure 1.1[23] Although the concepts in Figure 1.1 are often found in current literature on the economics of natural resources, their definitions and classification have not yet settled down. The concepts are presented in the figure from left to right roughly in declining order of clarity, operational usefulness or degree of acceptance by the economics profession at large.[24]

Direct use value arises from the use of the output of a good or service which has been the object of a transaction by intermediate or final consumers. Direct costs are the production costs of inputs which the producer or user incurs, including transport, distribution, etc. These elements, private costs and benefits constitute the core, and often the totality, of the elements that determine the supply and demand curves for resources. The indirect use values of resources include their indirect support and contribution to other economic activities or environmental services. In so far as some of these values are not appropriated by or charged to the user, they correspond to externalities.

Social opportunity cost also includes 'user cost'[25] i.e any costs that the present use of the resource imposes on future users.

With respect to exhaustible resources, user cost for any future period is the difference between the costs that users now have and those they would have had if the resource had not previously been used (Pearce, 1989, p.14), the cost imposed on future users by having depleted the resource. More generally, it is the reduction in the value of a resource due to using it as compared with not using it.[26] Like externalities, user costs correspond to indirect use values. They could be described as a particular kind of intergenerational externality.

Option value is the amount people would be willing to pay to preserve the option to use the resource in the future. Option value can also include the opportunity with time to gain information about the actual value of the resource. If the resource is destroyed, then the information base is to a large extent destroyed with it (Turner, 1991, pp. 60–1). Option values are on the border line between use and non-use values.

Non-use values include the opportunity to pass the resource on to future generations, allowing them the opportunity to benefit from it (bequest value). Lastly, people may attach value to the mere existence of a resource without wishing to use it or to reserve the option of using it in the future. There is an influential current of public opinion, often called ecocentrism or deep ecology, in which the biosphere and all its components have a right to exist in a sense an absolute value regardless of any instrumental value they might have (Leopold,1949, Schaefer-Guignier, 1990).

Social opportunity cost is simply the mirror image of non-use values. In so far as the resource is depleted, the remaining non-use values are diminished; this gives rise to corresponding opportunity costs.

Problems in Determining Resource Value

Determining almost all the elements of value shown in Figure 1.1 raises far-reaching problems. This section focuses on those involved in user costs and the bequest and existence values. Externalities are at the heart of PPP. They are discussed earlier in this chapter and in other parts of this volume.

User cost is a function of the value of the prospective additional yield which would be obtained at some later date if the resource were not used now (Keynes, 1936, p. 70). Keynes (1936, p. 73) had no doubt about the importance to resource policy of the concept of user cost:

> In the case of raw materials the necessity of allowing for user cost is obvious; if a ton of copper is used up to-day it cannot be used tomorrow, and the value which the copper would have for the purposes of tomorrow must clearly be reckoned as a part of the marginal cost.

Future prospects are essentially uncertain and the uncertainty grows the more one peers into the future. In so far as user cost reflects solicitude for future generations, the distance may indeed be long. Furthermore, as was pointed out above with respect to option value, the passage of time affords one the opportunity to gain information about the usefulness of the resource. If the resource is exhausted before this information is collected, no way remains of discovering, not to mention valuing, the unknown uses thus precluded.

On the supply side the foregoing could be described as uncertainties. On the demand side, sustainable development stresses 'the ability of future generations to meet their own needs'. Since future generations cannot of course tell us what their needs will be, we can only guess at them in a general way that is of little operational value. For example, they will undoubtedly need food, but what kind of food and how much? Alternatively, the present generation can impose needs on future generations. It has created concentrations of toxic and nuclear waste which future generations will have to monitor and manage. It is certain however, that the World Commission on Environment and Development was not proposing intergenerational imperialism when it formulated its definition of sustainable development.

Since it is logically impossible to determine an efficient market price in conditions of uncertainty, a non-market process must be used to incorporate user cost when taking resource policy decisions in the perspective of sustainable development. The Precautionary Principle comes into play in this context.

Assigning a figure to option, bequest and existence values is an exercise in counterfactuals; Rose (1992) presents a brief survey of valuation techniques. Notwithstanding the growing number of studies attempting to quantify the values, it is precarious to place too much weight on answers to questions of the kind 'you will not actually have to pay anything, but if you had to, how much would you be willing to pay for ...?'. In these circumstances, it is tempting and painless to quote a high price. 'A group in a society with a strong preference for environmental protection can easily take the position of a free rider in demanding an especially intense environmental protection if the group does not contribute to the costs of that policy' (Siebert, 1987, p. 142).

The free-rider problem would be acute if payment were actually required, because option, bequest and existence values all have characteristics of collective goods. If people wish to safeguard but not exercise their option to visit a national park, that option still remains available to others. Congested areas become an issue only if the option is exercised, at which time it ceases to be an option and becomes a direct use. Similarly, if people want their descendants to live in a world in which a particular orchid exists, it will also exist for the descendants of all other people. Option, bequest and existence values are collective goods and need to be dealt with through public policy like other such goods.

In short, a political process is needed to decide how much should be spent on conserving a resource or how great an opportunity cost will be accepted for forgoing its exploitation. The political process may result in the adoption of mechanisms which affect prices and thus influence resource use, but using prices is not the only choice available nor is it always the most effective one, as Heal points out in this volume.

The Users

Users can be divided into the following categories:

> (a) consumptive users
>> (i) quantity
>> (ii) quality
>
> (b) Amenity users
>> (i) active
>> (ii) passive.

Using water as an example, consumptive users may either consume a certain quantity, e.g. for drinking or irrigation, or they may reduce its quality by using its absorption capacity to dispose of waste and by-products, e.g. by discharging effluents into a river. Quantity and quality uses can be combined, e.g. by those who take clean water from the domestic supply network and return used water to the sewage network. Amenity users neither consume nor pollute the water. Active amenity users of a lake may swim or sail there. Passive users may simply admire its beauty.[27] Passive amenity uses correspond not only to the use values shown in Figure 1.1, but also to non-use values. It is often possible to bring the competing and complementary demands of resource users into play in such a manner that market prices are generated.

It is relevant to sustainable development that the rich give more importance to amenity uses and the poor to consumptive ones. Juhasz lists a number of North–South implications of UPP-based resource pricing.

A resource may be of only local environmental importance but still play a role in international trade, for instance as an input into a traded good. For instance urban water quality is a local environmental concern, but a low standard keeps down the cost of water used as an input in a factory producing goods for export to developed countries. The demand for water created by the demand for the exported product is thereby increased. This is no more than an expression of comparative advantage.

If the rich, especially the rich in developed countries, want a resource in a developing country to be conserved, they are simply amenity users according to the classification of users presented above. If the amenity demand is expressed in a higher price for the resource, a solution is thereby found for the conflict of interests. Let it be emphasized that we are now talking not about externalities but about the price of resources. For the payment to be effective in resource allocation, it should be paid to the owner, i.e. the party who is in a position to decide how the resource should be used. It follows that amenity users in the North should actually pay the owners of resources which are located in the South for the amenity they use. UPP is entirely consistent with side payments to developing countries of the type included in the Montreal Protocol on Ozone Depleting Substances. Those who wish to conserve the ozone layer are amenity users and those who deplete it are consumptive users.

If non-use values supported by the rich are expressed in higher prices for resources like water, land or fuel, thereby making it more difficult for the poor to meet their basic needs which depend on the consumptive use of these resources, the solution once again must be to ensure adequate income for the poor in the monetary sector or adequate guarantees of access to the resources for those outside the monetary sector. Juhasz suggests that subsidies may be justified on equity grounds, but points out that on efficiency and dynamic grounds they have the same drawbacks under UPP as under PPP. Part of a solution to this problem may lie in the allocation of property rights. If they are vested in those who have been using the resource, the property income they receive will help offset the higher price. It will also give the users a double incentive to use the resource in the most economic way: as consumers, they will be encouraged to consume less because of the higher price and as owners they will want to maximize their property income.

Property Rights

The authors of the essays in this volume were asked 'to look at the concept of PPP along with UPP in a broad perspective and to comment on the merits, drawbacks and technical feasibility for developing countries of applying these principles'. It is revealing that Geoffrey Heal focused immediately on property rights in answering this question. This is a key issue in both UPP and PPP and to environmental economics in general.

Property rights are pertinent with respect to North–South trade. As Chichilnisky (1991) has pointed out, the supply function of an environmental resource depends on the nature of the property rights for that resource and determines the patterns of trade. If there are no regulations or enforceable private property rights in a resource, the private cost of using it is relatively low. Since property rights regarding environmental resources are better established and enforceable in developed countries, the private cost of using them is higher than in a developing country. The supply of the resource appears to be abundant in the South because of the greater difference between private and social costs (Chichilnisky 1991).

With respect to PPP and UPP, in identifying the owner of a resource, one identifies who is responsible for looking after it. The owner has an interest in responding to economic incentives income due to the property or payments which must be made on its account. The owner is under an obligation to respect the legal or administrative rules that apply to the property. In short, the owner receives and responds to signals. If the owner is not correctly identified, the signals are weakened, distorted or simply lost.

Conversely, owners have an interest in defending their property. Those who directly use a resource get to know it well. Recognizing ownership rights in favour of the users is a way to ensure that information is used correctly, which is an aspect of the Subsidiarity Principle. In cases where management requires complex knowledge and experience at a local level, if there is a collectivity which has been exploiting a common property resource, then denying property rights to it can result in loss of output and consequent loss of welfare for the community as a whole, a movement away from the Pareto frontier. Even if a different ownership apparently increases total output, loss in income to less visible earlier beneficiaries may be ignored. Efficiency requires an estimate of both income gained and lost. In many situations this estimate cannot be achieved without consulting the traditional beneficiaries, who could be regarded as having been de facto owners.

The management of resources outside the market can be particularly important for the poor. Poor communities with little access to money often have sophisticated mechanisms for managing the resource base on which they depend. When the development process brings these non-market forms of resource use into competition with market uses, sustainable development, with its objectives not only of reducing poverty but also of safeguarding the prospects of future generations, needs to give full weight to 'traditional' forms of resource management.

While assigning property rights can play a major role in environmental policy, it does not follow that these rights should always be exploited through the market in the money economy. As Parikh points out, this can aggravate the conditions of the poor by exposing them to the greater financial power of others. Assigning property rights can be a way of protecting activities from the market which may in turn be environmentally sound. Environmental economics focuses on two problem areas with respect to property rights: common property resources and externalities. Some of the aspects relevant to development are noted below.

The need to specify the owners, their rights and their duties applies to common property resources. Regardless of whether they are preserved or abandoned in favour of 'modern' economic methods, existing ownership rights and duties often need to be clearly identified and if necessary redefined in the light of the challenges which development sets for resource management. An important issue in working out these rights is that resources may have multiple uses and that some of the uses can easily be reflected in market mechanisms while others cannot. Traditional commons like meadows, woods or coral reefs used to be the property of an identifiable collectivity. Right of access was restricted to members. Within the collectivity, social rules regulated use in the interests of the members and of the sustainability of the resource. Management failures can often be attributed to the misperception that the commons belonged to everyone, ownership being consequently vested in the State. The result was a loss of information as well as of incentives to manage the resource sustainably.

With respect to externalities, Coase (1960) establishes that whoever of the two parties concerned owns the rights has no influence on the ultimate optimum degree of pollution. The paradoxes which he exploits to literary effect arise because the reader is thinking not only of efficiency, but also of equity. Whoever holds the property rights determines who pays whom. This has an obvious bearing on income distribution. The overriding imperative of sustainable development seems to suggest that priority should be given to the poor in allocating the ownership of resources from which a positive income can be derived. To use Coase's example, if the foundry provides employment and income to poor workers, while the sanatorium provides rest and recuperation to wealthy people of leisure, property rights in the air, the noise-carrying medium, should be vested in the foundry.[28] Since ownership has no bearing on efficiency, policy considerations can be restricted to equity.

It is with this concern for equity that UNCTAD (1992) has developed its proposal for tradable carbon emission entitlements. The atmosphere can absorb only a certain amount of greenhouse gases. One way to control emissions is for the public authorities to fix an overall ceiling for emissions, and then allocate the rights among owners, who are free to trade them. Nothing is more global than the global climate: it belongs to everyone. The UNCTAD proposal therefore allocates ownership rights in proportion to population. From the point of view of efficiency this is as good as any other solution, but from the point of view of equity it generates a flow of funds in the form of payments for resource services rendered from the relatively small number of people in developed countries who emit large amounts of greenhouse gases to the more numerous and poorer populations in developing countries who emit less.

ECONOMIC AND OTHER TYPES OF MECHANISM

In general, economic efficiency and welfare are maximized when the marginal social opportunity cost of output and the marginal social welfare derived from consuming that output are equal. In many different circumstances, the operation of markets in a free-market economy can be expected to produce a reasonable approximation to this outcome. However, the growing awareness of environmental issues has brought to the fore important cases in which markets left to themselves will not maximize economic efficiency and welfare. This will occur whenever the full marginal social cost of production is not borne by the producer, or when the full range of marginal social benefits of consumption is not received by the producer of the output. These occurrences, or market failures, call for remedy by the public authorities. These remedies are either direct constraints on behaviour like command and control instruments, or a framework of constraints within which the market thus channelled better achieves social objectives; or again, government may itself be such an important economic agent that its own decisions on revenue and expenditure which can be called administrative measures, can influence the behaviour of the rest of the economy.

Public authorities have legal and regulatory or administrative measures at their disposal, which can, in the right circumstances, be designed so that economic measures come into play. In theory some forms of market failure can be brought into the sphere of economic mechanisms, but in practice legal and regulatory mechanisms may be preferable because of the cost or unreliability of economic mechanisms. In other cases, it is impossible to use economic mechanisms because there is no way of determining an appropriate price. Uncertainty in the strict sense is an example. It may also be impossible to ascertain the value that people really attach to collective goods, thereby necessitating compulsory payment through taxation and corresponding public provision.[29]

The aim of UPP is to function as an economic device: 'the implementation of pricing for resource use that reflects the full long-run marginal social cost of using the resource would promote economically efficient and environmentally sustainable use of resources'.[30] Nonetheless, its implementation needs to go beyond economic mechanisms. Firstly, it embraces PPP which, we have seen, is not an exclusively economic mechanism. Secondly, it is explicitly intended to include the costs of foregone future uses of depleted resources, which the market is unable to determine. OECD therefore concludes with respect to UPP that, as with PPP, 'the internalization of costs can be achieved through regulations and/or economic instruments'.[31]

The Precautionary Principle concerns uncertainty, which is unquantifiable, as opposed to risk, which is quantifiable through the calculus of probabilities. As a result, it is an inappropriate ground for economic mechanisms and calls for regulatory measures. These measures may be derived from game theory, a tool which, although known to some economists (and many decision theorists), is not a market mechanism. Chisholm and Clarke, in their chapter, more specifically investigate the circumstances in which the conservative minimax type of PP rule can be rationalized as a two-person game against nature.

The Subsidiarity Principle might be thought of as purely political, but it can find expression through the market. Buyers and sellers are the people most directly concerned by the good or service traded. The market for some goods is local because people further away are not interested in it; e.g. housing or local food specialities. These markets however, are often affected by geographically broader ones. In appropriate circumstances, allowing markets to decide can amount to implementing the Subsidiarity Principle in a more effective way than a political process.

In short, three of the four principles examined in this study PPP, UPP and SP can be implemented through either legal and regulatory or economic means (but economic means, of course, need a legal and regulatory framework). The PP can rely only on legal or regulatory mechanisms. The choice of means depends on the state of social organization,[32] i.e. on the strengths and weaknesses of the political and administrative structures in each case. OECD (1991a) suggests the following criteria for the choice of policy instruments.

> Economic instruments constitute one category amongst others of instruments designed to achieve environmental goals. They can be used as a substitute or as a complement to other policy instruments such as regulations and cooperative agreements with industry. In some instances, for economic and administrative reasons, direct regulation and control are appropriate when, for example, it is imperative that the emission of certain toxic pollutants or the use of hazardous products or substances be wholly prohibited. In other instances, economic instruments can supplement regulations in order to strengthen the enforcement of standards designed to protect public health.

The choice of environmental policy instruments can be made against five sets of criteria:

> (i)   Environmental effectiveness: The environmental effectiveness of economic instruments is mainly determined by the ability of polluters to react. The primary objective of economic instruments is to provide a permanent incentive to pollution abatement, technical innovation, and product substitution.
> (ii) Economic efficiency: In a broad sense, economic efficiency is achieved by an optimal allocation of resources; in a limited but more operational sense, it implies that the economic cost of complying with environmental requirements is minimised.
> (iii) Equity: Distributive consequences vary according to the types of policy instruments applied. For example, pollution charges or taxes entail additional payment on the discharge of 'residual' pollution; additionally their distributive impact would depend upon how the revenue is used. Similarly, with marketable permits, the distributional effects will differ according to their initial allocation.
> (iv) Administrative feasibility and cost: All types of policy instruments involve implementation and enforcement structures. This relates in particular to the ease and cost of monitoring discharges and the number of target groups involved and also upon the nature of existing legal and institutional settings.
> (v)   Acceptability: It is of crucial importance that target groups be informed and consulted on the economic instruments imposed on them. In general, the success of any (economic) instrument requires certainty and stability over time with respect to their basic elements.'

CONCLUSION

It would be rash to state that the universal application of PPP, UPP and PP would or would not benefit developing countries and the world's poor. The distribution of benefits depends on the following: how and at what level norms and standards are set; the degree to which the interests of all the parties concerned are reflected in these decisions; who produces goods, services and pollution and who consumes them; and who in the broadest sense owns the resources. All these issues may be negotiated under the three principles. To accept these principles does not close off any options for developing countries.

Furthermore, it is only fair that those who benefit from a good or service should pay for that benefit and that those who inflict harm should either pay to prevent it or pay the damage. PPP was designed with at least one eye firmly on avoiding distortions in international trade. The four principles discussed in this volume can serve this objective. It is very difficult for a country to create an appropriate environmental policy entirely on its own. Some harmonization is inevitable. 'Harmonization' has many meanings, encompassing such concerted actions as: (1) uniform policy (e.g. uniform taxes and standards); (2) agreement on common policy instruments (e.g. charges) but allowing each country the freedom to adopt its implementation and form; (3) agreement on common principles (like PPP), (OECD, 1991b, p. 89).

Strict uniformity may well be unnecessary and even undesirable. On the contrary, 'taking due account of diversities between different countries and regions is, in fact, an important condition for efficient environmental management, both at a national and an international level, since each policy must fit as much as possible into the environmental conditions, social preferences, and economic structures prevailing in each country'. (OECD, 1991b, p. 88). Given the basis for a diversity of environmental standards among countries, it is important to avoid solutions that are imposed by the larger or richer countries. 'When an environmental problem involves a transborder physical spillover, the only alternative to unilateral actions based on economic and political power is for countries to co-operate in the design, implementation and enforcement of an appropriate multilateral agreement for dealing with the problem at hand'. (GATT, 1992). Accepting principles which already have widespread legitimacy (like PPP, UPP and PP), can serve this objective by focusing the debate on the contentious issues of substance, only within a framework of agreed principles which are in themselves an important aspect of harmonization.

NOTES

1. The definition of sustainable development is given in the Introduction.
2. The phrase is borrowed from Annex 1, Recommendation, para.I.3, which concerns PPP. It applies equally well, however, to the other principles.
3. Annex 1, Recommendation, para. I.2.
4. Annex 2.
5. Annex 1, Note, para. 3.
6. That is indeed one reason why sustainable development insists on the overriding priority due to the essential needs of the poor.
7. More complex social and institutional arguments are needed to establish the degree to which PPP imposes burdens on rural poor with access to resources outside the market. This line is not pursued here.
8. Annex 1, Note, para. 2.
9. UNEP Governing Council, Decision 15/2, Annex II, May 1989.
10. Annex 1, 'Guiding Principles', para. 6.

11. Annex 1, Note, para. 2.
12. Annex 1, Note, para. 2.
13. The terminology is borrowed from GATT, 1992, pp. 29.
14. Annex 1, Recommendation, para. III.2.a.
15. This is clearly reflected in the Basel Declaration signed by 28 countries and the European Community on 22 March 1989, at the time the Basel Convention on the Control of Transboundary Movements of Hazardous Wastes and their Disposal was adopted.
16. Annex 1, Note, para. 8.
17. Annex 1, Recommendation, III.2.
18. Taking the phrase broadly rather than in the technical sense which PPP attributes to it.
19. See Annex 2, section 2.
20. Annex A, Note, para. 4.
21. *Ibid.*
22. Annex 2, section 2.
23. The following argument is based on Pearce (1989) and Turner (1991).
24. The ranking by degree of acceptance may well be different in other circles, e.g. among environmental militants.
25. It is unfortunate that the OECD should be giving currency to the terms both 'User cost' and 'User-Pays Principle', since the word 'user' has rather different senses in the two cases.
26. The fount of thinking on user cost is Keynes (1936), Chap. 6, 'Appendix on user cost'.
27. The foregoing classification follows that of the OECD: see Annex 2, section 3.
28. This is one possible scenario. Another is one in which the patients in the sanitorium are workers who have diseases of poverty while the foundry is run by an elite of well-paid technicians.
29. Notwithstanding Coase (1974).
30. Annex 2, section 4.
31. Annex 1, p. 1.
32. The definition of sustainable development includes 'the idea of limitations imposed by the state of ... social organization on the environment's ability to meet present and future needs'.

2. GUIDING PRINCIPLES FOR SUSTAINABLE DEVELOPMENT IN THE DEVELOPING COUNTRIES

Ferenc Juhasz

INTRODUCTION

Economic Trends in OECD and Developing Countries

Over the last 20 years OECD countries have had to reconcile and achieve simultaneously several economic and environmental objectives: reduce pollution, protect the natural resource base, maintain economic efficiency, generate economic growth, and ensure the orderly development of international trade and investment. To move towards these objectives at a reasonable speed, governments have followed certain economic principles for environmental protection and sustainable development of natural resources.

They implemented those principles with a range of regulatory and economic instruments, a restructured administrative framework and amended legislative and judicial arrangements. During this period of intense policy formulation and implementation Governments also experienced two major oil shocks which seriously impeded and complicated economic and environmental management.

During this period the OECD region almost doubled its GNP and OECD countries increased their trade threefold. These facts and other supporting data led OECD Ministers to conclude that economic growth and environmental improvements are compatible and mutually supportive (OECD, 1991a), and that existing policy structures are a good basis for integrated economic and environmental management facilitating sustainable development.

Can the OECD experience be transferred to developing countries using the same economic/environmental principles to formulate sustainable development and the same mix of economic instruments and institutional, legal and judicial arrangements? Recent evidence (World Bank, 1991) suggests that today even poor developing countries can grow much faster than OECD countries did at a comparable stage of development. (The United States needed 50 years from 1840 to double its per capita income; China did so in 10 years, from 1977). Consequently, there are good reasons to believe that the OECD experience can be replicated to some degree in many developing countries.

The main reason for developing countries to achieve fast growth is due to international trade: through trade they can import the means (goods, technology, ideas) to make their assets (labour, natural resources) more productive. Global linkages of the developing economies, together with a competitive microeconomy and a stable macroeconomy, are the basic ingredients of growth. The global linkages are: trade in goods and services, foreign investment and technology, and ability to meet world standards including environmental standards.

Criteria for Development in Developing Countries

As developing countries attempt to establish sustainable development policies (i.e. economic growth combined with pollution control and resource conservation) one of their main concerns is the impact of these policies on global linkages. Sustainable development can proceed only if these linkages are further developed; there is therefore considerable interest in pollution control and resource management policies that can ensure this. At the same time, it is understood that international trade and investment are highly dependent on microeconomic competitivity and macroeconomic stability.

Developing countries are under considerable internal and external pressures to undertake effective and far-reaching pollution control and resource conservation measures but at the same time they fear that these policies could undermine their growth prospects. There is little doubt that some of the Asian economies (e.g. South Korea, Taiwan, Singapore) and some Latin American countries (e.g. Chile) could successfully follow OECD environmental and resource management policies. There is some uncertainty, however, regarding sub-Saharan Africa and some Asian economies such as India.

The internal pressure for implementing environmental measures comes from the need to improve public health, to reduce the danger of major accidents and to protect and manage natural resources so as to ensure their long-term viability both from the national and international point of view. The external pressure comes from OECD countries, partly to ensure the protection of an internationally important natural resource base, partly to protect the health of their own populations and partly to ensure fair conditions for international trade.

This chapter examines the relevance of OECD principles and practices for developing countries, particularly those at the lower ranges of the income scale such as in sub-Saharan Africa.

Arguments have been advanced that throw doubt on the advisability of strict application of OECD-style principles and policies:

- developing countries cannot afford OECD standards because the cost of their implementation would destabilize their macroeconomic policies;
- even if they could afford these costs, their export industries need to be subsidized to keep them competitive in the world markets;
- sustainable development of natural resources is a world-wide concept and developing countries cannot and should not carry the burden of conservation alone.

These arguments have found considerable support not only in developing countries but also in OECD countries and they merit careful consideration. However, they need to be looked at in the context of the framework discussed above: fast growth has been achieved with the help of competitive microeconomic and stable macroeconomic policies (connected through the price system and financial discipline) and through global linkages. This suggests that environmental policies should work through the price mechanism (i.e. not through subsidies) and that natural resources should be priced at their social (i.e. including both economic and environmental) costs. The real dilemmas are in the global linkages which need to be protected from temporary disruption during the environmental transition period.

Criteria for Sustainable Development

Sustainable development is a world-wide issue but to some extent more relevant to developing countries than to OECD countries. Because of population growth, climatic conditions and world-wide demand for their natural resources, the economic and environmental bases of developing countries are in much more imminent danger than those of OECD countries.

The question therefore is: are the policies used by OECD countries sufficiently strong and immediate to arrest the decline in the resource base of developing countries. A brief answer is that developing countries need conservation policies even stronger than principles such as resource pricing could provide and that they also need substantial assistance to implement those policies and to maintain a 'reasonable' rate of economic growth at the same time.

OECD PRINCIPLES FOR SUSTAINABLE DEVELOPMENT

Rules for Combining Development and Environmental Protection

The OECD's work in the field of environment has concentrated mainly on evaluating and exchanging national experiences in pollution control, facilitating international cooperation in many areas, including transfrontier pollution control, promoting the ideas of economic efficiency in pollution control and advocating integrated resource management and sustainable development.

Consequently, many OECD recommendations have urged Member countries to develop regulatory mechanisms to control air, water, and noise pollution as well as waste. Others have suggested legal and administrative instruments to achieve specific environmental objectives. On the whole these policies and instruments aimed at achieving certain environmental objectives only. However, it was recognized at an early stage that all these measures had economic consequences and that on their own they could be counterproductive in the long run, e.g. by specifying pollution control technologies, thereby discouraging new technologies.

Simultaneously, other OECD recommendations argued for economic approaches to environmental policies, aiming specifically at minimizing the incidental economic costs of environmental policies and/or enhancing the economic benefits such as technological improvements. These principles, contained in various recommendations, set out well-recognized economic ideas such as the Polluter-Pays Principle (PPP) and the Resource Pricing Principle (also known as the User-Pays Principle, UPP).[1]

Another set of recommendations advocated greater use of economic instruments to implement environmental policies (OECD, 1991c). There are other OECD agreements which aim at minimizing environmental risks from certain products and at the same time influencing international trade, as in the case of chemicals and hazardous waste[2] (OECD, 1986a, 1986b).

These principles and instruments helped OECD countries reach a degree of economic growth, environmental quality and resource replacement which, together with technological progress, approaches the concept of sustainable development as presently interpreted.

The Polluter-Pays Principle

PPP has two principal objectives: (1) to promote microeconomic efficiency in the implementation of pollution control policies; and (2) to minimize the potential trade distortions arising from environmental measures.

These objectives are clearly interrelated and can be achieved largely through the allocation of the costs of pollution prevention and control, i.e. by internalizing into the cost of production and/or consumption the economic costs and part of the environmental costs (capital and operational costs of prevention and control, and residual damage) of the external effects (pollution). The polluter should bear the cost of pollution control; thereby market forces would bear on him to change his behaviour either by introducing new pollution control technologies or by changing production processes or production patterns.

As PPP was developed in an international context special attention was focused on the international aspects. These are discussed in detail, together with the domestic microeconomic efficiency and macroeconomic stability issues, in the guidelines attached to the Recommendation: subsidies, standards, non-discrimination, exceptions and implementation (see Annex 1).

Subsidies

According to PPP, environmental measures should not be accompanied by subsidies which would compensate for their cost. Non-subsidization should ensure that the price mechanism worked efficiently and that there would be no burden on the public budget with possible destabilizing effects. In this way distortion in international trade, created through different levels of subsidy, would be avoided.

Subsidies are defined as cash grants, tax benefits, accelerated amortization, or credit facilities. In the longer run, they fail to bring about a reduction in pollution. In the short run they are more effective in reducing pollution, but inefficient because they increase the total cost to the community, and unfair because they transfer the burden to the taxpayer. Internationally they could lead to competitive subsidization and subsequently to distortion. In 1974, the OECD Council reaffirmed the non-subsidization concept and recommended that PPP be observed.

An extension of the non-subsidization concept is the prohibition of compensating import levies and export rebates, or measures having equivalent effects to offset price differentials (Annex 1, Guiding Principles, para. 13). If allowed, these would protect domestic industries from the price differentials due to pollution control. The same arguments about lack of incentives, inefficiency and unfairness apply to these levies or rebates as they do to subsidies.

Quality and emission standards

PPP is not specific concerning environmental standards. It addresses national standards and harmonization of standards among OECD countries. Regarding the level or severity of standards it speaks of ensuring an acceptable state of the environment (Annex 1, Guiding Principles, para. 4). It addresses the extent of the need for harmonization of environmental policies (Annex 1, Guiding Principles, paras. 6–8).

In setting standards it is left to member governments to decide the acceptable level and tolerable amount of pollution, with the intention that environmental policies should not disturb microeconomic efficiency and macroeconomic stability. If the cost of non-subsidized pollution prevention and control cannot be absorbed without unbalancing efficiency and stability, standards need to be adjusted.

Concerning harmonization, PPP accepts different national standards according to different assimilative capacities, different social objectives and different degrees of industrialization and population density. However, it urges harmonization with respect to timing and scope of regulations so that certain industries can avoid unjustified disruption of international trade patterns.

In the same context, PPP states that environmental measures should avoid creating non-tariff barriers. For internationally traded products, governments should seek common standards and agree on the timing and general scope of regulations for particular products. This has become a contentious issue and has led to delays in implementing product standards in some countries and also to delays in introducing technological innovations, i.e. to inefficiencies.

National treatment and non-discrimination

PPP also states that in conformity with GATT provisions there should be national treatment, i.e. identical treatment for home-produced and imported polluting products and non-discrimination between imported goods regardless of their national origin. The term 'polluting product' is not defined and can be interpreted as polluting during production, consumption or disposal. This section has recently become important and is used to protect home products from polluting imported products which pollute more.

Rules for exceptions

Under PPP, the following exceptions are allowed when government assistance is given to polluters for pollution prevention and control costs if:

- socio-economic problems could develop that would negate the environmental policy objectives;
- the assistance serves research and development;
- the measures are intended to avoid serious interregional imbalances and if they have the incidental effect of constituting aid for pollution control;

then subsidies may be given provided that they:

- are for existing plants;
- are selective and restrictive;
- are limited to well-defined transitional periods;
- do not create significant trade distortions.

Assistance to new plants should be given only under conditions that are even stricter than those for existing plants.

Rules for implementation
The PPP Guidelines are not specific regarding the implementation of PPP. In the Note to the Recommendation it is suggested that it could be implemented by a variety of means, ranging from process and product standards or regulations on individual pollutants to pollution charges.

Regulations are proposed for speedy pollution reduction or in cases where the nature of the pollutants or the number of polluters make pollution charges less effective.

Charges should be used in the framework of a comprehensive policy to:

- achieve objectives at the lowest social cost;
- provide continuous incentives;
- finance collective facilities.

Resource Pricing (The User-Pays Principle)

Resource pricing is a well-known and well-accepted economic principle of long standing. It has been used for various renewable and non-renewable resources. However, the proper price to be charged for the resource was never clearly established and the price for the same resource often varied by region.

Recognition of environmental concerns added special emphasis to resource pricing:

- environmental costs associated with the exploitation and use of the resource needed to be included in the price;
- resource pricing could influence the use and conservation of the resources;
- there are connections between PPP and resource pricing.

The principle
Resource pricing as part of environmental policy-making was first introduced in 1987 in the 'pricing of water services' and subsequently adopted by OECD countries in 1989 as part of the integrated water resource management policies;

this was later generalized in the Ministerial Communiqué in 1991 (OECD, 1991a)

The findings of the 1987 report on water pricing:

> supported the general applicability of the 'User-Pays Principle' recognising at the same time the historical and social background of Member countries. The essential element in the User-Pays Principle is that an incentive is provided for the user to economise the use of the service or the natural resource. The user would pay the full cost, and this is similar to, and indeed embraces, the more familiar PPP. By imposing the economic and environmental cost as the price the use of the resource would be limited to economically and environmentally acceptable level (see Annex II).

The 1989 Recommendation on Water Resource Management Policies, referring to 'resource pricing' (and not the User-Pays Principle) stated that 'effective water management policies should be implemented, amongst other measures, through appropriate resource pricing for water services'. The Appendix to the Recommendation provides more detail. It maintains 'that resource pricing should be the main economic instrument and should be used for all types of water services'.

The 1991 Communiqué by OECD Environment Ministers gave full recognition to resource pricing and urged its use as part of environmental policy. The Background Paper submitted to Ministers advocated its use for water, forest and land resources (OECD, 1991c).

The pricing rule

Firstly, the pricing rule proposes that in the case of renewable resources the price should cover not only the resource itself but all the various services associated with the resource which cease to be available if the resource is used up or overused.

Secondly, the price should be the opportunity cost including the capital, operation and maintenance of providing the resource, the depletion cost and various environmental damage costs associated with the provision of the resource. These costs should reflect the long-run incremental costs to the community of providing the resource, i.e. the long-run marginal social cost. The principle clearly states that the authorities, in formulating the pricing structure, should take into account not only economic efficiency but also environmental and conservation objectives.

Exceptions to the rule

Financial subsidies as a whole, for particular groups of users, or between groups, should be justified on equity grounds. Subsidies might be considered separately for different resources. For example, in the case of water the subsidization of low-income groups through higher prices to other producers might be justified.

In some cases long-run marginal social cost pricing could lead to substantial surpluses for the producers, which might be used to rectify residual environmental damage or to subsidize particular groups of users.

Resource pricing and PPP

The 1987 OECD report on Pricing of Water Services (OECD, 1987a) states that under the User-Pays Principle the polluter remains responsible for the cost of pollution and prevention control; it suggests that these two principles should be applied in an economically efficient and coordinated manner, but this needs to be further evaluated.

Control of Chemicals

The work of the OECD on chemicals and the various Council Decisions and Recommendations concentrate on international agreements aiming at minimizing potential damage from chemicals to human health and the environment. This is to be achieved at minimum economic cost, particularly with minimum disruption to international trade.

As stricter rules are being imposed on the quality and use of chemical products, internationally accepted rules are being used to facilitate world-wide trade in these products. These rules cover such areas as internationally accepted good laboratory practices, mutual acceptance of data, and safeguards for the confidentiality of these data. Without these agreements, testing new and existing chemicals for their human health and environmental acceptability would have to be carried out in each Member country but would still not necessarily be accepted by other countries. These OECD agreements are therefore particularly important for international trade between OECD countries and should be widened to include non-OECD countries so that discrimination in international trade can be avoided.

Hazardous Wastes

The OECD Recommendations on Hazardous Waste aim at ensuring that hazardous waste is disposed of in the manner required by national regulations in OECD Memberaid countries. One objective is to deal with trade in hazardous waste between countries. Such trade should be carried out transparently with proper certification so that authorities in both the exporting and receiving countries are fully informed of the quantities and exact nature of the waste products concerned in each case.

An aim of the Recommendations is to limit trade in hazardous waste to countries which have the proper disposal facilities. This will ensure environmentally acceptable disposal of highly toxic materials. It will affect trade with developing countries by reducing revenues from such trade until technology and funds from OECD countries are transferred to them to create the disposal facilities.

OECD Guidelines for Multinational Enterprises

Environmental protection
These guidelines have been accepted by OECD governments with the objective of regulating the behaviour of multinational enterprises in both OECD and non-OECD countries. In particular they aim at ensuring that multinationals are subject to the same environmental health and natural resource regulations as are domestic companies. The guidelines propose the use of technologies and practices compatible with these objectives as well as the introduction of systems of environmental protection.

The Environmental Guidelines are supplemented by Guidelines for Science and Technology which require the rapid diffusion of technology and granting licences for the transfer of technology. These transfers are important for environmental protection both in OECD and developing countries.

APPLICATION OF THE PRINCIPLES IN OECD COUNTRIES

During the first 20 years of environmental policies the macroeconomic performance of OECD countries was creditable. There is no evidence that economic growth, inflation, international trade and balance of payments have been adversely affected by environmental policies. Similar conclusions can be drawn concerning microeconomic efficiency and improvement in global linkages. There have been significant improvements in all these areas and the way environmental policies were implemented did not hinder these improvements.

Efficient Use of Natural Resources

Certain elements relating to the implementation of PPP indicate that it was adhered to in the following ways:

- subsidies provided by central governments for environmental purposes were a small fraction of total pollution control expenditure;[3]

- in a number of countries governments successfully used PPP and their international obligations to resist demands by industry for pollution control subsidies;
- there is no evidence that environmental policies led to significant distortions in international trade;
- in countries with strict environmental standards, low subsidies and a high degree of dependence on international trade, technological progress in pollution control was rapid and profitable (e.g. the motor vehicle industry in Japan).

However, there are still considerable differences between OECD countries in their interpretation and application of PPP.

Standards
Until recently there have been significant differences in emission and ambient quality standards; even where standards appeared to be similar their implementation varied substantially. In some countries, where standards are applied on a plant-by-plant basis, it is not feasible to verify actual emission standards. More recently, particularly in EC countries, standards have converged and probably helped to avoid trade distortions.

Subsidies
Even though data suggest that subsidization had not been significant, the actual level of subsidies might be understated because governments treat the data in different ways:

- financial assistance from central to lower levels of government and subsequently passed on to industry or households has not been accounted for and the amount is not known; nor is the amount provided directly from the funds of lower levels of governments;
- 'hidden' subsidies are implied and in fact provided under schemes where pollution charges fail to cover the full costs of pollution control services; the costs are partly covered by the general budget; no estimates of these 'hidden' subsidies are available;
- there are revolving funds created originally for environmental purposes and refinanced from loan repayments and donations which are also often used for subsidization;
- there are so-called 'self-financing' systems, where charges are used to collect revenues, which are redistributed to firms in the same industry; the non-transparency of this type of scheme led to an international debate regarding its conformity with PPP;

- in other cases potential polluters are subsidized through charges on the potential beneficiaries; e.g. farmers are subsidized for loss of production arising from reduced polluting activities in water protection areas;
- subsidies are often provided for waste treatment including recycling activities.

From the environmental point of view some of these subsidies may have been beneficial in that they speeded up the implementation of regulations, but they probably delayed the introduction of new technologies. Consequently, their microeconomic efficiency is suboptimal and discriminated between firms and industrial branches.

The overall judgement is that the OECD countries could still significantly improve the implementation of their environmental policies by reducing further the wide range of subsidy schemes and improving their transparency.

Experience with Resource Pricing

Resource pricing in a limited form has been a practice in all OECD countries since the 1950s. However its application has been of limited use from the environmental point of view. Firstly, resource prices failed to reflect the external costs associated with exploiting, transforming and using the resource together with the costs of forgone future uses. Secondly, even when prices reflected some of these costs users were unable to respond to prices because of non-transparencies in the system like absence of meters in the use of water. Thirdly, because there was no clear definition of property rights, users were difficult to identify.

A further limitation on the implementation of resource pricing in OECD countries is that environmental authorities in most countries have no control over natural resource policies and in some of the countries integrated management operates only to a limited extent.

Another difficulty is the apparent overlap between PPP and resource pricing. Some authorities use this as a pretext to postpone action.

Pricing the resource

Textbooks suggest that the price for the resource should be the long-run marginal social cost. While the concept is relatively simple there are major difficulties in calculating all its components. The introduction of environmental considerations has further complicated these calculations.

In principle, the environmental costs for each resource need to be enumerated separately for the following categories: external cost associated with exploitation (e.g. in the case of water the construction of collection dams), delivery (e.g. construction of pipelines), use (e.g. depletion, transformation, crowding,), disposal (e.g. pollution, salination, waterlogging). These costs need to be quantified and evaluated before they can be incorporated into the price. Some suggestions for evaluating environmental cost have been made but need to be more widely accepted at the international level (OECD, 1990).

Another major problem with the calculation and evaluation of the long-run marginal social cost is the definition of 'long-run' for environmental purposes. Regarding certain natural resources, e.g. tropical rain forests, the policy might be long-run preservation i.e. there should be no diminution in the quantity and no change in the quality of the resource. In these cases the price should reflect these severe constraints and lead to a very low rate of exploitation of the resource. OECD practices lead to either a total ban on exploitation (and, in turn, to the use of resources from developing countries) or immediate but imperfect replacement of the resource (in the case of wetlands) representing a high price of the resource.

Application of the price
When the price, or a range of prices, for a resource is established its application requires an appropriate institutional framework and appropriate techniques. Even where the institutional framework, political will and public support for implementation exist, the technical requirements are costly. In the case of water this would for example consist of metering and frequent billing. This needs to be done so that the user can respond rapidly to the cost and price changes. Even in OECD countries, metering is not always available, and not at all for water sources on one's own property.

In some areas metering and charging might not be necessary until capacity is reached in use, e.g. recreational use of forests or waters. But even in such cases there is usually some low-level damage accumulation and administrative costs which should be charged for.

Resource ownership or, who is the user?
In many areas resource pricing is difficult to apply because of the disputed ownership of the resource. Even in relatively simple cases, such as water, ownership in many countries is not clearly defined. To give a few examples: in countries where all water resources are state owned there are disputes between the central and provincial governments as to ownership and the right to impose a charge; in most countries groundwater rights are poorly defined and landowners claim a free right to abstract a certain amount of water; rights to use privately owned wetlands are often subject to dispute between the state and the private owner; use of rivers and lakes for non-consumptive uses are legally not well defined and therefore charging is difficult, e.g. for power plants.

Even more complex issues arise in cases where the quality of water is subject to use. Who has the right to the natural state of water: the so-called owner (without clear title to water ownership) or the final consumer? As mentioned earlier, in one German state a farmer who claims the right to pollute groundwater under his property is compensated for his 'losses' (due to foregoing polluting activities) from taxes imposed on the final water consumer. This is the case in which PPP and resource pricing are mixed with a lopsided interpretation of PPP.

Resource pricing and environmental protection

Until recently environmental authorities approached the question of natural resource management and resource pricing with great hesitation and suspicion. There were several reasons for this caution:

- with few exceptions environmental agencies have no direct natural resource policy responsibilities;
- natural resource management and the use of pricing mechanisms were regarded as 'unethical' in certain environmental agencies;
- in most cases only pollution control and clean-up operations were regarded as the proper functions of environmental agencies; the preventive aspects of good husbandry of natural resources were not understood.

This situation has now changed (OECD, 1985). In principle the importance of resource management for the environment has been recognized but the appropriate mechanisms still need to be put in place.

PPP and resource pricing

PPP is used in OECD countries for efficiency and cost-effectiveness in pollution control measures. Resource pricing is used for efficient use of natural resources and to minimize the environmental impact of the use of these resources.

Resource pricing is in fact the User-Pays Principle but an OECD expert group (Group of Economic Experts) could not agree on the definition of UPP. The argument used against it was based on poorly defined property rights: PPP would imply that the polluters of the Rhine water would accept their obligation for the clean-up costs.[4] Another delegation argued that the UPP would allow polluters to pass on the cost of pollution control to the final users of the water. For these reasons it was thought advisable to avoid the term 'User-Pays Principle' and use the more neutral 'Resource Pricing'.

A more solid argument was that the various relationships, particularly the overlap between UPP and PPP, have not been explored and clarified. In fact the overlap usually occurs if the same instruments are used for implementation, as is the case with user charges advocated as economic instruments for pollution control as well as resource pricing. There are however even in this case well-defined and fundamental differences.

Polluter charges are used, particularly in the case of water pollution, as incentives but more often as revenue-raising instruments for financing public waste-water treatment facilities. Water for public consumption is usually treated as potable water. Under PPP, pollution treatment cost is recouped from polluters (households, industry, agriculture). Under UPP, water treatment costs for potable use, as distinct from pollution treatment costs, are, or should be, charged to the user.

Under PPP, charges for disposal of waste are imposed. Charges for cleaning up waste dumps to restore a natural resource (land) are also pollution charges. However, under UPP, other charges related to land, e.g. restoration of land around dams, are charges on natural resource use and come under UPP. Product charges are pollution related and therefore come indirectly under PPP.

As a rule one might argue that charges, fees, taxes, etc. for pollution-related activities (air, water, noise) are imposed as economic instruments consistent with PPP and aims to avoid subsidization that would be inconsistent with it. On the other hand charges imposed for the consumptive use, damage or destruction of natural resources, (land, water, forests, wetlands, coastal waters, marine resources, wildlife, etc.) are imposed under UPP or resource prices with the aim of ensuring their efficient use or preservation.

Current application of resource pricing
Resource pricing in many forms is widely used in OECD countries but there are very few cases where most of the external costs are incorporated in the prices, for example, certain nature protection zones and water pricing in some areas of the US and Australia.

In addition to the technical dificulties, calculating prices and metering, there has been opposition from user groups which enjoy substantial subsidies and from development agencies responsible for managing the resource.

Government policies in many sectors are undermining efforts for good resource management through resource pricing by subsidizing resource-using activities. Agriculture is one of the prime examples of such subsidization. By subsidizing the agricultural sector directly or through tariffs and import quotas, governments subsidize water use, draining of wetlands, soil erosion and desertification. For UPP to be effective, subsidization of resource-using activities needs to be reduced or abandoned.

APPLICATION OF OECD PRINCIPLES IN DEVELOPING COUNTRIES

Successful pollution control and above all resource management policies leading to long-run sustainable development are crucial for developing countries. While these policies contribute to welfare improvements in OECD countries, some argue that in developing countries they are essential for their survival (World Commission on Environment and Development, 1987).

It is even more important in developing countries than in OECD countries that these policies achieve their environmental and conservation objectives and improve economic development to reduce poverty and introduce improved health and population control policies.

The introduction of these policies to be able to bring them towards sustainable development implies fulfilling the following complex mix of criteria:

- improve the environment;
- ensure long-term efficient natural resource management;
- improve microeconomic efficiency and competitiveness;
- maintain macroeconomic stability;
- develop global linkages;
- achieve equity requirements.

It will be very difficult for developing countries to achieve all these objectives simultaneously in the short or medium term to ensure long-term sustainability. The degree of success will largely depend on implementation and on the principles used to guide implementation.

Suggestions are made below for environment and resource management priorities which developing countries might consider and how the OECD principles might be used to achieve them, keeping in mind the countries' economic and equity requirements. These priorities and requirements are divided into the following categories:

1. Environment/resource management priorities:
   - efficient use of natural resources;
   - public waste-water treatment;
   - air pollution control: energy production and use;
   - integrated pollution treatment: major industry complexes.
2. Economic priorities:
   - global linkages;
   - microeconomic efficiency;

- macroeconomic stability.

3. Sharing the cost burden:
    - polluters/users;
    - developing and OECD countries.

In the following pages the two OECD principles are assessed. Each environmental/resource management objective is discussed separately and with the help of PPP and UPP the impact of their achievement is assessed for the other (economic and equity) objectives.

Exhaustive Use of Natural Resources

In the management of natural resources, three major environmental issues are involved:
- exhaustive exploitation;
- preservation of ecosystems;
- quality deterioration.

Exhaustive exploitation can be avoided by management that will ensure the long-term survival of natural resources. Forests and marine resources are the best examples. However, as is now becoming evident, the present rate of exploitation of these resources in developing countries is rapidly exhausting them. Some observations about this type of exploitation are noted below:

- a high rate of exploitation occurs to speedup economic development;
- in some cases exploitation of a resource is replaced by other economic activity (forests by agriculture);
- exploitation of resources in developing countries helps conserve similar resources in OECD countries;
- exploitation of certain resources could lead to world-wide environmental impacts, e.g. with tropical rain forests;
- overuse of the resources can lead to economic losses in the medium term;
- exhaustive exploitation could affect the economies of other countries, e.g. marine resources.

The question is how and to what extent the application of UPP together with PPP will achieve the above-mentioned environmental and economic objectives within the constraints on some of the resources. Different resources will respond differently to UPP; the market structure will also be decisive for the effectiveness of pricing policies.

Given these caveats and the difficulties described above in calculating resource prices, it is evident that general observations about the effectiveness of UPP will need to be substantiated by specific studies.

Preservation of ecosystems is an integral function of several natural resources and can be achieved only by strictly regulating their use. Developing countries often have large areas which contain unique ecosystems, yet the loss of trade and income from them could be severe. When these ecosystems are of world-wide importance, developing countries might need to be compensated by OECD countries for the income forgone due to preservation.

Quality degradation that occurs through pollution or inappropriate use (e.g. soil pollution or erosion) might be dealt with with the help of PPP and UPP and restored with low-level state support. It is unlikely that there would be trade losses or other economic impacts from these corrective policies. However, continuous neglect could lead to significant economic losses and natural disasters.

Environmental effectiveness of pricing

The national environmental effectiveness of resource pricing will be strong in non-traded resources such as water, because pricing can be easily introduced. With internationally traded resources (like timber) environmental objectives could still be achieved, but only if price imposition can be ensured through international agreement binding all producing countries. Pricing still may have to be supplemented with taxes and royalties to impose clear economic signals on the producers. Similar arrangements should also be imposed on land even though it is not traded internationally (OECD, 1991c). International environmental objectives probably can also be achieved, e.g. to minimize climate change, but the price adjustment would have to be significant and applied internationally; for example with carbon taxes or tradable permits. High international prices for some of these global public goods are preferable to an import ban, such as on tropical timber, because a ban would reduce their value and thus their maintenance; it could increase the transformation of forest areas to other activities, e.g. agriculture.

To facilitate the effectiveness of the price mechanism, measures, in addition to development taxes and royalties, are also needed. When other parts of the economy are seriously distorted through subsidies and similar interventions by governments the effectiveness of resource pricing is reduced.

Economic effectiveness of pricing

Global linkages and pricing. Receipts from the sale of these resources on the export market will depend on the elasticity of international demand and on the observance of international agreements on pricing these resources. In the short run receipts sharing is likely to increase until the market declines through replacement, e.g. with home-grown timber from OECD countries.

Foreign investment in these resources can decline over a period in expectation of declining demand, but this can be reversed by a licensing (concession) policy which favours long-run sustainable developers.

Developing countries may be able to maintain or even increase their trade receipts and investment flows if they can bargain for greater access into OECD countries for processed products from their resources. In any case, trade and investment effects are likely to be less serious in response to a pricing policy than in response to a prohibition on exploitation, even if the prohibition were coupled with compensation from OECD countries.

The effectiveness of pricing, however, will depend heavily on how the pricing policy is implemented, e.g. taxes, guarantee bonds, tradable leases coupled with management conditions, etc. In addition, pricing policy will have to be supplemented (depending on the resource) by:

- management training;
- development activities by international organizations, e.g. FAO, World Bank, etc., that are not counterproductive;
- allocating concessions in a way which supports long-run sustainable development.

Microeconomic competitivity.   From the point of view of microeconomics, pricing of natural resources will restore efficient allocation particularly if it is supported by a gradual elimination of sectoral subsidies (e.g. in agriculture) which counteract resource pricing.   In both the OECD and developing countries, different forms of sectoral subsidies are provided to support production. These lead to overuse of natural resources (e.g. water for irrigated agriculture, forest land for agriculture, overfishing, etc.).   Eliminating these subsidies is an essential element of effective pricing policy.

Some restructuring between agriculture, forestry, fishing and other resource-exploiting and using industry will be necessary and so the change has to be gradual to avoid sudden economic and social dislocation.

Macroeconomic stability. The Overall price level will be marginally affected as these resource products usually form only a small component of the overall price index.

Governmental budgets are likely to receive a positive impact from increased royalties, concession fees, development taxes, etc; furthermore, expenditures on subsidies will decline.

Unemployment might increase marginally in some regions during the adjustment period.

Sharing the cost burden

Avoidance costs of exhaustive exploitation should in principle be borne by the user. This could be achieved through the various charging systems in addition to international contributions to ease the burden of potential economic effects.

The costs of ecosystem preservation could be shared between developing and OECD countries or paid for largely by OECD countries, depending on the international significance of the ecosystem or the distribution of activities leading to its destruction.

The costs of controlling deterioration of quality would largely be governed by PPP but in developing countries equity would require a broader sharing of this burden through general tax revenues.

Public Waste-Water Treatment

In terms of human health, waste-water treatment and clean drinking water would produce the greatest benefits and significantly contribute to increased life expectancy. Waste-water treatment would improve water for drinking and for industrial, agricultural, recreational and other purposes. It would require canalization and treatment plants. They are now available only in a few of the largest cities in the developing world, but even then only primary treatment capacity is usually available and the rate of connection to users is low.

The cost of public waste-water treatment both for industry and households is financed by public authorities and consists of substantial investment, operation and maintenance costs. In OECD countries canalization construction costs are \$US800 per metre and \$US1200 per inhabitant equivalent for chemical treatment (primary, physical treatment costs are about one-third of this figure). The amounts for a major city are substantial and even in OECD countries only primary treatment facilities are available for 30 to 97 per cent of the population; secondary and tertiary treatment facilities are provided for a much smaller segment of the population (OECD, 1991d).

To provide sufficient waste-water treatment for a significant section of the urban population in the developing world in the foreseeable future would require expenditures beyond these countries' capacities. Yet the environmental and health benefits would be of great value.

In OECD countries most of these costs are charged to the polluters in a large part of industry and households, in tune with PPP. In principle the same practice could be applied in developing countries although the poorest segment of the community would probably have to be subsidized.

Environmental effectiveness of waste-water treatment

From the national point of view, the environmental importance of waste-water treatment is great and has many different benefits. As was the case in OECD countries this should be the first priority in developing countries in pollution control together with clean drinking water. From the international point of view waste-water treatment is important in internationally-shared water resources (rivers, lakes, groundwater and coastal waters). The OECD countries have considerable interest in some coastal water areas such as the Mediterranean.

Economic significance of waste-water treatment

Global linkages. These can be affected through the need for foreign capital to finance treatment plants and the subsequent repayment obligations in foreign currencies. Funds can be raised from the international lending agencies but environment authorities often have difficulty obtaining permission for such loans from their own finance ministry or central bank. Developing countries need low-interest loans and schemes to repay in local currency in order to start a significant waste-water treatment programme.

Microeconomic competitivity. Economic efficiency and competition of firms paying charges under PPP should not be affected; charges under the public treatment system are relatively low and would absolve firms from charges of unfair competition.

Macroeconomic stability. The main obstacle to the implementation of a major and rapid programme is macroeconomic stability. Given all the demands developing countries are facing in their public sector, strict budgetary discipline is necessary. Under PPP, these systems should be self-financing in the long run, but in the early stages borrowing requirements are high.

Sharing the cost burden. With PPP the cost burden is borne by the polluter. Subsidies can be granted to the very poor for equity reasons. International assistance might be given through low-interest loans and repayment schemes in local currency.

Air Pollution Control: Energy Production and Use

Air pollution generated by energy production and use are the major components of total air pollution in both urban and rural areas. The major stationary sources (e.g. power plants) are relatively easy to handle technically but retrofitting can be expensive. Retrofitting smoke-gas desulphurization with electrofilters costs about $US400 per kW which corresponds to $US4 billion for 10,000 MW.

New power plants with built-in pollution control cost about $US 1,600 kW or $US 16 billion for 10,000 MW; (corresponding to West German emission standards).

Application of PPP would require that the additional cost of pollution control be paid by the electricity producers and, ultimately, if they are to operate profitably, by the users. The increase in the cost of electricity will depend on many factors (the industry's profile, use of primary energy, capacity use, etc.) and a general calculation cannot be made.

However, calculations available for OECD countries suggest that those energy price increases would add substantially to the cost of production of energy-intensive industries and could affect their ability to compete with imported products, or to export.

Environmental effectiveness of air pollution control–energy

In industrialized countries over 50 per cent of air pollution (SO_2, NO_x and CO) is generated by fossil fuel combustion; that situation is likely to be similar in developing countries with some variation. The environmental effectiveness of controlling power plant emissions is high for the following three reasons: firstly, the plants are usually situated close to large population centres and therefore a reduction in emissions would benefit a significant proportion of the population; secondly, power plants have a long operational life; thirdly, pollution control can also result in energy savings and therefore is economically important. In most cases pollution reduction can also be achieved by changing the raw energy inputs, e.g. low sulphur fuels and coal washing, which can result in more rational exploitation of energy resources.

Global linkages. Exports and imports could be affected in a number of ways: higher cost electricity would add to the cost of production; importing cleaner fuels would add to the import bill; and pollution control technology may have to be imported.

Recent examples from aid provided to Central and Eastern Europe suggest that OECD countries and the EC are willing to provide assistance for energy production pollution control associated with economic benefits from energy savings.   Drawing on this experience international aid perhaps could be expected in this area for developing countries also, particularly as the electricity supply is such a vital ingredient of development strategy.

Microeconomic competitivity. Sound energy pricing is sound development policy and therefore pollution control costs should be internalized in the price of energy to consumers, particularly in industrialized countries. Within an electricity price structure there are however sound economic reasons for providing off-peak or very large consumers with differentiated prices, as well as for cross-subsidization within the industry. On equity grounds also there are good reasons for providing certain sections of the community with subsidized prices provided they do not distort competition.

Macroeconomic stability. OECD studies suggest that the implementation of PPP helped rather than distorted the stability of the macro-aggregates, which is likely to happen in developing countries as well. Experience suggests also that international borrowing is acceptable for pollution control in the energy sector.

Sharing the burden
In the energy sector two types of distributional arrangements may be acceptable: (1) some shift of the cost from the poorest segment of society to electricity users at large; (2) intergovernmental assistance from the OECD and large petroleum-producing countries to developing countries.

Integrated Pollution Treatment–Major Industry Complexes

Pollution control in industry in developing countries needs to be applied selectively depending on: the type and age of the plant; its location; costs; and economic impacts. Based on such considerations pollution control could be concentrated on a limited number of industries (plants) which pose major health and environmental threats in specific regions.   Concentration of pollution control in a few areas and on major industrial complexes could be particularly effective if they are undertaken in an integrated way including the whole life-cycle of substances and products and the various environmental media. Pollution control could be given priority according to the quantity and harmfulness of waste. Such an approach would make the products of these industries acceptable on a global basis.

   This advanced approach is advocated for developing countries for several reasons. Recent experience from OECD and Central and Eastern European countries suggests that retrofitting of old industrial installations is no longer profitable given that available new technologies are already incorporated into new plants.

Environmental effectiveness of integrated pollution control

The approach would have significant environmental benefits only in the medium term. These benefits would however be distributed throughout all environmental media and in the order of their danger to human health and the environment. In the medium term, environmental regulations will be required for new small enterprises for which there is currently no technical alternative.

Economic effectiveness of integrated pollution control

Global linkages. The policy proposed here would not impose any major cost burden on existing industries and therefore would not affect exports. As a declared policy for new installations, it would lend respectability to the environmental approach in developing countries and therefore to their export products.

The main issue is how new foreign investors would respond to this policy which would require them to use the latest technology. Available evidence suggests that it would not necessarily alter investment intentions.
Subsidies to export industries could be still granted under PPP if strict regulations are imposed on old existing plants.

Microeconomic competitivity. Under this policy, industry would only be marginally effected in the short run. Industrial restructuring with built-in environmental controls would significantly improve the competitiveness of new industries. This could attract new capital and new foreign investment.

Macroeconomic stability. As there are no significant subsidies or major governmental expenditure programmes involved, the macroeconomic impacts are likely to be negligible.

Sharing the burden

The main burden under this scheme is that of the immediate environmental benefits forgone. Should developing countries decide that they have to implement more ambitious environmental programmes for industry they would have to limit subsidies to crucial (export) industries to avoid the other negative economic effects. It is unlikely that foreign funds could be attracted for pollution control in domestic industry.

ASSISTANCE FOR THE APPLICATION OF OECD PRINCIPLES

The pollution and natural resources problems of developing countries are well documented and recognized as serious to the extent that they retard these countries' development and endanger public health.

OECD countries have been urging immediate action to remedy the situation. Environmental standards, corresponding to WHO norms need to be imposed to protect health and even more stringent standards are needed to reduce the economic damage due to pollution. To protect world heritage and climate, drastic action in developing countries is also needed in natural resource management.

In 1989 per capita income in low-income countries was $US330 as compared with $US19,000 in OECD countries. For reasons of economic self-interest as well as on equity grounds, there are strong arguments for environmental assistance to developing countries.

Such assistance is more likely to be forthcoming if developing countries can develop a gradual programme dealing with health and economic needs, taking into account the interests of OECD countries as well, and based on OECD principles. Both OECD governments and their multinational enterprises have a role to play in these assistance schemes.

Bilateral and Multilateral Governmental Assistance

In the protection of natural resources OECD governments individually and through international agencies can provide funds for preservation or selective exploitation of internationally important resources, tropical forests, wetlands, etc. Various schemes are already in operation, e.g. debt-for-nature swaps, and can be extended to cover various forms of debt on a much larger scale, provided that OECD governments are prepared to play a more positive role.

Through their own commercial policies OECD governments can impose tariffs on some natural resources from developing countries and then use the revenue to 'purchase conservation'. They need to reinforce their supervision of projects financed through international governmental lending which in the past ignored sustainable development requirements. They could could also impose development royalties on some of their own natural resources to promote their conservation and transfer the receipts for 'conservation purchases' in developing countries.

For pollution control a more liberal lending policy is needed both on a bilateral and multilateral basis, particularly for treatment of waste water and drinking water. Earmarked low-interest, long-term loans repayable in local currency are essential to implement such a programme. This could be supplemented with technical assistance in building and operating such plants, also on a long-term basis. Twinning arrangements could be established between river basin agencies in the OECD and developing countries for managing major rivers on a sustainable basis both for quality and quantity.

For air pollution control and efficient energy use, OECD countries could transfer both their technical and management expertise to developing countries as part of their assistance programmes. To avoid waste and duplication, this could be organized through an international agency such as the OECD International Energy Agency.

Multinational Enterprises

Multinational enterprises are users of the resources of developing countries and sell their products in these countries; in many cases they have established major production facilities in developing countries and regard them as the major markets for future developments. They are mutual partners today and this partnership will grow in the future. It is in the interest of multinationals that these markets grow rapidly for products already sold in OECD countries. OECD multinationals have already agreed to 'take appropriate measures in their operations to minimize the risk of accidents and damage to health and environment and to mitigate adverse effects'. They will use the appropriate technologies, introduce a system to protect the environment, including environmental auditing, implement education and training, and prepare contingency plans. The OECD Guidelines for Multinational Enterprises apply to all countries in which these enterprises operate (OECD, 1986b).

Consequently, they are obliged to implement local regulations, follow the OECD Decisions on Chemicals and implement the Agreement on Transport of Hazardous Waste. Legally, multinationals are expected to act in developing countries as they do in OECD countries. It is up to the governments in these countries to enforce this requirement.

However given the economic interests of multinationals in developing countries it is in their medium-term interest to use the advanced technologies of integrated pollution control everywhere in the world, and to observe the same product standards.

This self-policing mechanism might be reinforced by monitoring their operations through international agencies which would publish the results. There is already a measure of voluntary control through major investment funds which screen companies for their environmental performance.

If developing countries need to provide inducements for multinationals to invest in them they need to provide incentives other than environmental. It has always been argued that low environmental standards were never an inducement for investment in developing countries.

CONCLUDING REMARKS

This chapter argues that developing countries are in urgent need of major but prioritized and staggered environmental programmes and efficient resource management to move towards sustainable development.

Based on the achievements of the OECD countries, this chapter suggests that OECD principles and instruments could also be employed successfully in developing countries. Four areas – natural resource management, waste-water treatment, air pollution control from energy facilities and integrated pollution control for major industrial facilities – were suggested as priority action areas. The application of OECD principles, PPP and resource pricing, or UPP, were examined in these areas according to three broad criteria: environmental effectiveness, economic efficiency (global linkages, microeconomic competition, macroeconomic stability) and burden sharing.

The outcome of this brief analysis is that with some adjustments the OECD principles would in fact speed up the progress towards sustainable development. The main adjustment would be in the form of assistance required from OECD countries, particularly for policies in developing countries producing world-wide benefits.

NOTES

1 See Annexes 1 and 2.
2 'Transfrontier Movements of Hazardous Waste', 1984 and following Recommendations in particular the so-called Basel Convention on the Control of Transboundary Movements of Hazardous Wastes and their Disposal, 1989.
3 OECD Surveys 1976-1986.
4 Group of Economic Experts, 42nd Session, 1988.

3. IMPLICATIONS OF THE POLLUTER-PAYS AND THE USER-PAYS PRINCIPLES FOR DEVELOPING COUNTRIES[1]

Holger Bonus

INTRODUCTION

The Polluter-Pays Principle (PPP) and the User-Pays Principle (UPP) are both sound rules that basically serve the same purpose, namely to help restore the price mechanism in cases where it fails to work appropriately due to externalities or the character of environmental resources as public goods. Since distinguishing between these principles may in practice lead to ambiguities, it may help first to consider the meaning of these principles within a working market system.

I. ON SHADOW PRICES

Prices on ideal markets are 'shadow prices'. Given Pareto optimal resource allocation, shadow prices reflect the value of either a marginal commodity unit or a resource's marginal product. If shadow prices are actually charged on the market, then a Pareto optimal resource allocation will result from individual utility and profit maximization. In a formal sense, shadow prices emerge as Lagrangean multipliers from binding constraints to welfare maximization. Such a shadow price indicates the welfare loss arising from marginally tightening the respective constraint. For instance, when the supply of bread is limited, this amounts to a constraint, and the shadow price of bread then makes explicit (in terms of currency per unit of bread) the satisfaction forgone as a marginal piece of bread is taken away from the total supply, such that the overall constraint gets tighter and someone else has marginally to restrict his or her own appetite for bread. The shadow price reveals what the person who is thereby affected would be willing to pay for the missing bread. In fact, all consumers are individually responsible for removing bread from the total supply, and by having to pay the shadow price of bread, they are confronted with the welfare loss they inflict on others through their consumption. Consumers are thereby in a position to judge for themselves whether or not their own wishes can live up to those of others in terms of willingness to pay.

While the shadow price of a commodity accounts for the utility forgone by claiming commodity units for personal consumption, the shadow price of a resource reveals what is forgone in terms of alternative production when a resource unit is put into productive use. If the (marginal) unit were not devoted to its present use, it could be used efficiently elsewhere and would thereby generate a marginal product whose value is indicated by its shadow price. By having to pay shadow prices for the productive use of resources, resource users are enabled to judge for themselves whether or not their own use is efficient: if the resource cannot earn its own shadow price in its current allocation, then its use is wasteful, and the user faces a financial loss reflecting the value forgone by inefficient resource allocation.

In both cases, the shadow price can also be interpreted as representing the marginal social opportunity cost of economic activities. (Social costs, as contrasted with individual costs, embrace all costs resulting from an economic activity regardless of who is to bear them). If a commodity unit is claimed by one consumer, it cannot be claimed by another; its forgone utility must therefore be treated as a social cost. If a resource unit is put to use, it cannot be used for another productive activity, and its unused potential output constitutes a social opportunity cost.

Within the context of a working market system, PPP and UPP amount to one and the same principle. Both hold that consumers as well as resource users are to pay the shadow prices of their respective activities so that they will be confronted with the social opportunity costs associated with their decision to use commodities or productive factors. If their activities entail pollution, in a market environment they will either own the polluted medium themselves and be accountable for damages inflicted to their property, or they will have to obtain permission from affected owners and remunerate them for negative effects imposed. If their activities involve resource use, they will again own resources, or buy their services at shadow prices.

Let us now suppose that the detrimental environmental side-effects of economic activities are external in the sense that they are not contracted for, and adequate payments are not made. In this case the Polluter-Pays Principle requires that the polluter should face the same outlays as he would have without externality. In as much as pollution is involved, the polluter must be charged the shadow prices of polluting. The User-Pays Principle requires the same as far as (external) use is made of environmental resources: again, shadow prices are to be charged. Thus even in the case of externality, PPP and UPP amount to the same rule, provided that the depletion of exhaustible resources is properly shadow-priced using a social rate of discount. One should keep in mind that the social opportunity cost envisaged by PPP is, of course, to be understood as a long-run cost. Viewed in this light, there is no point in determining the implications of PPP versus UPP for developing countries, since both mean that social opportunity costs are to be met by polluters and resource users alike. From an economic point of view, there is no difference between utilizing environmental resources by means of discharging pollutants or wastes on the one hand, and using scarce environmental resources for services on the other.

II. TWO APPROACHES

One point should be made, however, with regard to internalizing environmental externalities via PPP (or UPP). There are two different ways to approach this end, and both must be weighed against each other.

The first (model I) amounts to evaluating the marginal willingness to pay of those adversely affected by a negative externality. When successful, such internalization yields a Pareto optimal status as it would have emerged, had the externality not been present, from individual preferences and production technologies. A natural resource, then, is evaluated according to consumer demand or to its marginal productivity. In a formal sense, (technological) externality is introduced into the analysis by inserting the externality-generating activities of third parties as arguments into the individual utility or production functions of those concerned. If PPP (or UPP) works, then the resulting quasi-market solution corresponds to the solution brought about through supply and demand in the absence of (Pareto-relevant) externality.

However, such a solution may not be suitable because it may ignore crucial ecological limits. We cannot in all cases afford to let the market, or a quasi-market, determine the quality of the environment, because the resulting solution might not properly respond to the need to maintain ecological equilibrium. To avoid environmental disruption, a certain minimum of environmental quality may have to be maintained regardless of consumer preferences. The second way of treating the environmental side-effects of economic activity (model II) is hence to add quasi-technological constraints to welfare maximization that will, if binding, command shadow prices of their own. For example, we might find that on a world-wide scale the emission of carbon dioxide must be quantitatively restricted. This would add a global constraint to be met jointly by all emitters of carbon dioxide, and PPP (as well as UPP) would require the development of mechanisms to charge CO_2 emitters the full shadow price of discharging carbon dioxide into the atmosphere.

Thus, when considering the institutionalization of PPP (or UPP) one must decide whether model I or model II should be followed. As a rule of thumb, the stricter model is to be selected. If the quasi-market solution (model I) called for more than minimal environmental quality, then there would be no reason not to let consumer demand for environmental quality have its say, because consumers would have indicated their willingness to pay the higher shadow prices associated with restricted utilization of the ecosphere. PPP (and UPP) would then determine consumers' marginal willingness to pay at Pareto optimal levels and charge polluters and users correspondingly. If, on the other hand, ecological restrictions call for standards tighter than those generated by means of a quasi-market solution, then ecological constraints are to be superimposed on consumer preferences (model II). This situation is similar to one in which children are excluded from the labour force for reasons of health and education, which means that the supply of labour is reduced and its shadow price raised beyond that of a pure market solution. Cases of this sort should be put before the electorate and decided in parliament. In all likelihood, voters would accept a proposition that would call for standards to be set in such a way that environmental disruption would be avoided. If model II were to be employed, then PPP (and UPP) would seek ways to identify the shadow prices of using restricted resources and would charge them to polluters/users. It should be noted that the Pareto optimum and shadow prices referred to in model I are different from those aimed for by model II.

III.   THE COASE THEOREM APPLIED TO UPP

As stated above, both PPP and UPP boil down to one and the same sound rule and would result in identical policies. However, the distinction between the two principles is fundamentally well taken when UPP is reinterpreted according to the Coase Theorem to reflect the reciprocal nature of 'harmful effects,' as the Nobel Laureate states it (Coase, 1960; 1988).

Costs are an economic, not a physical category. It is therefore necessary to distinguish carefully between these when it comes to identifying the social cost of a given arrangement. Often the physical source of an externality is clear cut; for instance, persistent noise bothering the residents of a sanatorium may stem from a nearby foundry. Physically there is no doubt as to the cause of the noise. The foundry is readily recognized to be the polluter and should hence be held responsible, according to PPP, for the cost of pollution control and preventive measures. From an intuitive point of view, it appears obvious that the foundry is at fault: if the foundry were removed, then there would be no noise damage.

However, the process of creating economic damage from noise generation is more complex than its physical counterpart. If, for example, the sanatorium were absent, there would be no noise damage. To cause noise damage, it takes not just a source of noise emissions, but a receptor that is susceptible to noise and may be harmfully affected. Thus the emitting plant and the adversely affected sanatorium are both parties to the generation of damage. While the causation of physical noise is due to the source alone, that of noise damage is not. The social cost of noise emissions originates from both source and receptor in a symmetrical way.

To see this point more clearly, imagine that the foundry had been at its current site for many decades before the sanatorium was built in its vicinity, attracted by low real-estate prices. In this situation it is easier to acknowledge that the sanatorium may be just as much the cause of noise damage as the foundry.

The social (opportunity) cost of an economic activity is defined as the value that is forgone by choosing one particular alternative; it consists in the loss of the highest-valued option resulting from this choice. The choice pertinent to the present example is one of two alternative uses of the local air mantle, which can be utilized: (1) as a medium of silence to accommodate the needs of the sanatorium's residents; or (2) as a carrier for the disposal of noise waves generated during the foundry's production process. Due to the pervasive nature of noise waves, the local air mantle cannot be used for both purposes at the same time, and thus deciding for one option amounts to waiving the other. Economic efficiency requires that the option seized should be (marginally) valued at not less than the most-valued option forgone, because the cost would otherwise be excessive. To determine the social cost of the arrangement, we must hence identify and compare the value of both alternative options.

Now suppose the willingness of the sanatorium's residents to pay for silence exceeds the benefits the foundry derives from its location. Then the most valuable use of the local air mantle is silence, and it is this use that should be chosen. This will be achieved if both the foundry and the sanatorium are faced with the true cost of their respective economic activities, as demanded by PPP.

If PPP is adopted as a guideline for environmental policy in this situation, then the foundry is held responsible for noise damage and must provide financial compensation to the sanatorium for residents who leave due to the noise. According to the above assumption, such compensation will exceed the advantages associated with the foundry's location, which in turn will cause it to relocate rather than compensate the sanatorium. In the end, PPP has succeeded in helping ensure that the local air mantle is put to its most valued use. Of course, this solution is to the advantage of the party that was physically harmed, and places the cost burden on the polluter. Note, however, that transaction costs are not accounted for in the present example.

But now consider a redefined version of the User-Pays Principle. The sanatorium demands an alternative utilization of the local air mantle that would fit its own needs, but which would also require the foundry to discontinue its use of the same resource. Why not let the sanatorium pay for its demand so that it will be confronted with the full social cost of its wishes? If the sanatorium holds that the present use of the local air mantle for disposal of waste noise should be replaced with amenity use, then it should be charged for such resource use.

Suppose the redefined UPP were adopted. Then the sanatorium would have to pay the shadow price of using the local air mantle as an amenity. In the context of that example, this shadow price would equal the value forgone by discontinuing the foundry's activities at its present location. By assumption, again, the sanatorium is in a position to meet the shadow price of amenity use because its residents value silence more than the foundry values its own location. Consequently, the same result as before emerges. The redefined UPP has thus done its job to put the local air mantle to its most valued use.

To be sure, switching from PPP to a redefined UPP induces a redistribution of wealth, and this in turn might affect the willingness of either party to pay. It is now the polluter who benefits, and the cost burden is placed on the party harmed physically. Also, of course, transaction costs may modify the outcome. Yet the main result of the Coase Theorem applied to environmental protection should not be ignored lest a broad field of policy options be abandoned. One can put environmental resources to their most valued use in two different ways which place the cost burden on different parties. Thus, by deciding for either PPP or a redefined UPP, one can take care of distributional concerns that might otherwise preclude the efficient allocation of environmental resources. For instance, when the polluter is poor and cannot meet the cost of pollution control and prevention measures, this would rule out application of PPP, but not application of the redefined UPP, which in principle is no less efficient than PPP but places the cost burden on the 'richer' party.

To complete the argument, consider what would happen if the sanatorium's residents were not as willing to pay for silence as the foundry was willing to pay for the value of its location. Then the most valued use of the local air mantle would be for disposal of waste noise. Suppose that PPP is adopted. Then the foundry would have to compensate the sanatorium for its loss of patients. Assuming this situation, the foundry can do so without the need to relocate, since the advantages it derives from its location exceed the willingness of the patients to pay for silence. Under these circumstances the foundry would continue operating at its original site, while the sanatorium would relocate.

If instead of PPP, the redefined UPP is adopted as a guideline, then it is up to the sanatorium to compensate the foundry for its relocation costs. By assumption, however, the sanatorium will be unable to do so because its patients value silence less than the foundry values its location. Thus, again, the foundry will remain, while the sanatorium will have to relocate. The result is the same as it was with the application of PPP, assuming that transaction costs or distributional effects do not alter the outcome. Thus both PPP and UPP result in the same quasi-market solution.

IV. INSTRUMENTS

In section II of this chapter it is stated that efficient allocation of environmental resources needs not involve the internalization of externalities (model I), but may use constraints instead that command shadow prices of their own (model II). It was recommended that if the standards emerging from either model differ, then the stricter of the two should be selected.

In practice, though, one may have to settle for less. Thus in paragraph 4 of the OECD's 'Guiding Principles'[2] (Annex 1), PPP is defined as the 'principle to be used for allocating costs of pollution prevention and control measures to encourage rational use of scarce environmental resources'. The text then goes on to elaborate that PPP 'means that the polluter should bear the expenses of carrying out ... measures decided by public authorities to ensure that the environment is in an acceptable state.' Thus it is not necessarily sustainability that directs public authorities when defining standards, but political and economic feasibility as well.

Yet the standards that are determined in this way nevertheless form binding constraints, and PPP, as viewed by OECD, would therefore postulate that each polluter be charged the shadow prices of such constraints. However, standards make sense only when many parties are involved. Thus spontaneous market solutions, as in the previous example, must be ruled out for now while we concentrate on developing the proper institutional devices that would bring about the required result: shadow prices applicable to polluting activities.

Although there are several instruments for achieving this goal (see, for instance, Opschoor (1991) and Barde (1991)), for the purposes of this discussion, three broad categories will suffice. Given the challenge of global warming due to greenhouse gases, and of ozone-layer depletion due to trace gases including chlorofluorocarbons, the focus will be on standards aimed at developing quantitative overall limits for certain pollutants, notably carbon dioxide. The three categories of instruments are:

- direct regulation;
- charges;
- transferable discharge permits (TDPs).

Direct regulation, or the 'command-and-control' approach, is certainly the most widely utilized institutional device for enforcing environmental policy. Polluters are notified as to what they may and may not do; consequently, the range of legal options is narrowed. It is by now clear that this category of instruments is economically inefficient because they neglect to account for the distribution of marginal abatement costs. Much more could be done for the environment if more attention were paid to this factor. But direct regulation is, moreover, also inefficient from an ecological viewpoint, because it is difficult if not impossible to design regulations that meet constraints on a macro level. The problem is that attainment or non-attainment of quantitative restrictions at a macro level (not more than x million tons per year within region y) emerge as a result of numerous individual decisions. Regulations are supposed to aim at macro conditions, but end by addressing only micro units. What kinds of command must be conveyed to individual households and businesses in order to generate individual emission patterns that add up to overall loads that meet the global standards?

Direct regulation is *inconsistent with PPP* because polluters are not confronted with the marginal opportunity costs associated with their decisions. Shadow prices are nowhere articulated in the process and the result is that the market fails to reflect the relative scarcity of environmental resources. People cannot react to scarcity and must therefore be forced to act according to decrees.

But direct regulation appeals to intuition and is therefore politically feasible. When restrictions are not global but of a strictly local nature, and when the transaction costs for implementing economic instruments are high, then direct regulation can be a superior measure. In some developing countries, and particularly in the states of the former Soviet Union, the legal and institutional prerequisites for economic instruments are not well established. In such cases, direct regulation may be the only available option. PPP would then imply that efforts be made to change this whenever possible.

The category of charges as economic instruments of environmental policy is best represented by Pigovian taxes, which would internalize Pareto-relevant externality (but leave Pareto-irrelevant externality). However, what we are dealing with here is not model I (see section II above), but model II, i.e., making the polluters pay the shadow prices of environmental constraints as determined by public authorities.

Charges (for instance for effluents) are economically efficient: they minimize the social cost of whatever pollution-abatement is performed after the charge has been levied (which assumes that charges are to be paid on the quantity of pollutants discharged). Pollution-abatement measures that would cost the polluter more than the charge levied on emissions are not implemented, while abatement measures that cost less than paying the charge are implemented. As a result, high-cost solutions are filtered out and total abatement costs are minimized.

The trouble with charges is that the shadow prices of the relevant overall constraints are unknown. The typical charge will deviate from the relevant shadow price; this means that polluters are not confronted with the marginal opportunity cost they cause. (If the constraint is to bind, then the marginal quantity emitted by one polluter cannot be emitted by another, who must therefore install abatement systems). Consequently, the overall constraint is not met, which in turn calls for the intervention of public authorities and more direct regulation. Since shadow prices change over time (in ways unknown to administrators), and since tax-rate modifications are extremly difficult to achieve politically, the chances of actually charging shadow prices to polluters are nil.

Charges are in accordance with PPP inasmuch as they succeed in confronting the polluter with costs, and thus in providing incentives for reducing emissions. Even if the rates charged are too low and fail to reflect marginal opportunity costs adequately, the economic efficiency of charging is a great advantage. In many cases, charges offer the best reflection of the ideal envisaged by PPP.

Transferable discharge permits (see Tietenberg, 1980; Joeres and David, 1983) establish quantitative overall constraints that specify an annual quantity to be legally discharged by the holder for a given pollutant. Permits are made transferable (within limits) and may be devalued when quantitative constraints need to be tightened. The market price of permits reflects the shadow price of the corresponding constraint and thus the polluter faces the marginal opportunity cost of his decision to emit pollutants. This mechanism allows PPP to be met in an ideal way. In case of charges, the price which a polluter is to pay for discharging one unit of pollutant is set beforehand, and it is then left to the market to determine the total quantity discharged. When transferable discharge permits are used instead, the overall limit is fixed in advance, and it is left to the market to determine the prices that polluters must pay. The shadow price of an overall constraint, which is unknown in the case of charges, is transformed into a market price by this instrument.

Needless to say, difficulties may arise from regional and local situations when a TDP solution is to be implemented. Pollutants whose spatial diffusion tends to be slow require the attention of public authorities; 'hot spots' must be ruled out through local injunctions, which in turn raise the transaction cost of the solution. No such difficulties exist, however, when global pollutants are to be controlled; it does not matter, for instance, at which locations the discharge of carbon dioxide is either stepped up or reduced, as long as the overall constraint is met. In the case of this gas, absorption characteristics should also be considered. Given a global ambient quality standard on CO_2, the additional absorption of carbon dioxide by growing trees, for instance, would expand the environment's assimilative capacity with respect to CO_2, and thereby generate options to emit more CO_2 without violating the standard. In such a case, opportunity costs are negative: one might think of granting additional CO_2 permits free of charge to those whose activities absorb significant quantities of carbon dioxide. Under a system of ambient permit systems, gasoline produced from recently grown organic matter might thus be considered a candidate for (partial) exemption from CO_2 permits for automobile fuels.

By far the greatest impediment to adopting transferable discharge permits is lack of political feasibility. While permits to utilize the environment as a medium for waste discharge are implicit even in command-and-control strategies (which, after all, permit the emission of pollutants once legal prerequisites are met), the explicit definition of 'rights to pollute' is intuitively unappealing and therefore runs into problems with voters, legislators and administrators alike. Also, the concept is difficult to implement in economies that lack the fundamental requirements for the establishment of markets; developing countries may not qualify. In such cases, hybrid concepts that combine elements of TDPs with direct regulation may be of great help in approaching PPP (see, for instance, Bonus, 1984 and Tietenberg, 1985).

So far, we have considered to what degrees instruments of environmental policy agree with PPP. What about the User-Pays Principle? The redefined UPP, applied to a system of charges, would require that subsidies be paid to polluters for reducing discharge levels. Similar to the sanatorium that compensates the foundry for closing down (section III above), the users of clean air or water may be envisaged, as it were, as paying for what they consume. As has been shown, this may be as efficient as the adoption of PPP. Qualifications have to be made, though, to avoid blackmail: polluters might be induced to step up polluting activities (or threaten to do so) only to qualify for compensation. Under a system of transferable discharge permits UPP would call for a different initial distribution of property rights than PPP. Using the foundry–sanatorium example again, PPP would call for the issue of amenity rights to the sanatorium's residents, which the foundry would have to buy before being entitled to emitting noise, while UPP would call for the sanatorium to purchase noise permits from the foundry in order to ensure silence for its patients.

V. APPLICATION TO THE DEVELOPING COUNTRIES

Let us now address the implications of PPP and UPP for developing countries while restricting discussion to world-wide CO_2 emissions. In 1985, carbon dioxide discharges resulting from the burning of fossil fuels amounted to 20.5

billion tons world-wide (Walbeck and Wagner, 1987; and also Fritsch 1990, Chap. 4.4). Out of this total, 28 per cent of emissions were produced in North America, while only 4.6 per cent came from Central and South America. The African Continent contributed a mere 2.8 per cent. The United States, the former Soviet Union and China jointly discharged 53 per cent of the total. World-wide, per capita emissions averaged 0.82 tons in 1960 and 1.08 tons in 1987 (Flavin, 1989). But the data exhibit large variances: in 1987, per capita emission was 5.03 tons in the United States, 4.24 tons in Canada, 4 tons in Australia, but only 0.03 tons in Zaire, 0.09 tons in Nigeria, 0.19 tons in India and 0.38 in Brazil. If world-wide per capita emissions continue to grow at current rates, then an average of 3 tons per capita can be expected within the next two or three decades, which, applied to an estimated population of 9 billion human beings, would mean that the present discharge of carbon dioxide will have quadrupled (Fritsch, 1990, p. 216).

The lesson to be learned from these data is that it would be a hopeless task to reduce CO_2 emissions world-wide through universal implementation of PPP. If developing countries are to grow, they will have to emit more, not less, carbon dioxide. This increase will have to be counterbalanced by drastically reducing the consumption of fossil energy in industrialized countries. The adoption of PPP in developing countries would mean that their growth would be precluded because of lack of currency.

However, the redefined UPP (section III) would work without loss of efficiency. This principle would interpret the present situation the other way: since the industrial countries inflated the world-wide discharge of carbon dioxide on a large scale in the past, it is now up to them to reduce their emissions in order to enable developing countries to grow without violating overall constraints on CO_2 emissions. From section III it should be understood that to look at the problem this way is no less legitimate than traditional PPP thinking.

In practice, it is doubtful that either PPP or UPP can be implemented in developing countries at the micro level by establishing national or local markets for transferable discharge permits. Institutional, legal and political conditions will not allow this in most cases. Charge/subsidy systems might fare better but in many cases command-and-control measures might be the best one could do. Often, however, there may be traditional, non-monetary forms of managing environmental resources in developing countries, which are of a religious nature; such ways of respecting natural limits and the interests of future generations should be encouraged.

Things are different at the macro level. An international conference might be authorized to develop binding national carbon dioxide discharge quotas. On which basis? One possible solution would be 'grandfathering', i.e. preserving the status quo by allocating quotas according to present discharge data. But such a solution would never be accepted by developing countries. These would plead for a per capita base instead, say, one ton per capita. That would curtail the United States to one-fifth of its present discharge volume while allowing India to emit twenty times as much as it currently does. Of course, the United States figure could not be met, while India could not possibly waste enough energy to increase fivefold its carbon dioxide discharge. However, national quotas could be made transferable; then the industrialized countries could buy parts of national quotas originally assigned to developing countries. This would lead to a huge influx of capital from industrialized into developing countries and would at the same time induce both groups to search for more efficient ways of generating and consuming fossil energy. Holding CO_2 emission quotas would amount to holding internationally convertible assets of high and lasting value. If the absorptive capacity of tropical rain forests was factored in by raising national CO_2 quotas accordingly, there would be strong incentives not to waste those forests for returns as negligible as a couple of years of extra grain harvests. While on the international level transferable discharge permits might prove a powerful instrument for promoting world-wide application of the (redefined) UPP, charge systems are less promising at this level due to national inflation and the associated lack of convertiblity of many national currencies.

NOTES

[1]   This chapter focuses on the Polluter-Pays Principle and the User-Pays Principle, as described in Annexes 1 and 2.

[2]   The formulation used in paragraph 2 of the OECD 'Note on the Implementation of the Polluter-Pays Principle' (see Annex 1) suggests, though, that the standards issued aim for a Pareto optimum according to model I. 'The notion of an "acceptable state" ... implies that ... the advantage of a further reduction in the residual social damage involved is considered as being smaller than the social cost of further prevention and control.' This would mean that remaining externality is supposed to be Pareto irrelevant, which in turn means that the resulting state is Pareto optimal (see Buchanan and Stubbeline, 1962, pp.371–84). This is at variance with the OECD's own interpretation that PPP 'does not involve bringing pollution down to an optimum level of any type'. (*ibid.*)

4. APPLICATION OF THE POLLUTER-PAYS PRINCIPLE IN DEVELOPING COUNTRIES

Geoffrey Heal

INTRODUCTION AND SUMMARY

The Polluter-Pays Principle (PPP) is an attempt to correct misallocations resulting from external effects by imposing Pigovian taxes and subsidies. As such, it is a theoretically valid approach and has a certain political appeal. A weakness of this approach is that consideration is rarely given to the issue of how to dispose of the tax proceeds in a manner that is non-distortionary. This issue is certainly not addressed by the OECD in its work on PPP. It seems unaware of the difficulty there is in specifying ways of using tax revenues that do not themselves lead to distortions, distortions which could in principle undo the corrective work of the Pigovian taxes. In addition, PPP neglects other potentially valid approaches to the correction of externalities, namely the definition of property rights and the allocation of quotas or tradable permits. The property rights approach in particular, although it cannot be endorsed generally, has the advantage of administrative simplicity, which may be of importance in developing countries. Also, the allocation of quotas, although again not generally endorsable, is preferable under conditions of uncertainty about cost and benefit functions when there may be significant non-linearities or threshold effects in either of these.

One form of environmental problem that is particularly important in developing countries is the common property resource problem or 'problem of the commons'. It is thus important to evaluate PPP and the alternatives in terms of their ability to correct inefficiencies arising from the 'problem of the commons'. Judged by this criterion, PPP does not emerge as a uniformly preferred approach. Revision of property rights or allocation of quotas may be preferable under certain conditions. Recent research indicates that differences in property right regimes, with respect to common property resources, can be important determinants of patterns of international trade, so that the treatment of common property resources assumes major significance in the context of a country's international strategy.

PPP AND COMMON PROPERTY RESOURCES

Many of the environmental problems in developing countries involve common property resources. Examples are: fisheries used as domestic food sources and as sources of exports; hunting grounds used for domestic food production; forests used as sources of firewood; aquifers as sources of drinking water and irrigation; the atmosphere as a sink for waste products; rain forests; grazing lands, rivers. An extensive enumeration and description of common property resources can be found in Dasgupta (1982), who emphasizes that they are frequently of great importance in developing countries. The issue is also addressed by Parikh in this volume, Chap. 5. A key question is therefore: Is the Polluter-Pays Principle acceptable in the face of common property resources in developing countries?

In a common property resource problem, there need not be a 'polluter' in the strict sense. The structure of the problem is as follows. There is a resource to which many have access, such as a fishery accessible to everyone with boats and nets, or common grazing land to which all members of a social unit customarily have access. Each user of this resource interferes with the use of the resource by others. When a new fishing vessel enters the fishery, some of its catch may be incremental catch, i.e. fish that would not have been caught if the vessel had not entered. But much of the catch may be fish that would otherwise have been caught by other vessels already fishing in that fishery. There is thus a negative inter-user externality, with one fisher catching in part that which in his or her absence would have been the catch of others. A similar analysis applies to common grazing land. The addition of another animal may lead to the consumption of some grass that would not otherwise have been eaten, but it will also deprive other animals already there of grass which would have been theirs. This negative externality between users can be thought of as arising from inadequately defined property rights. The standard analysis (Dasgupta and Heal, 1979, Chap. 3) indicates that in this case a misallocation of inputs arises because each user of the common property resource allocates inputs to the use of this resource until the marginal cost of inputs equals their incremental return to him or her. This incremental return is in fact the average productivity of the input in the exploitation of the common property resource. Hence inputs are allocated until marginal cost equals average product, and on the assumption of diminishing returns to inputs in the exploitation of the common property resource, this implies that the resource will be used beyond the point that is economically efficient. Figure 4.1 is a simple illustration of this point.

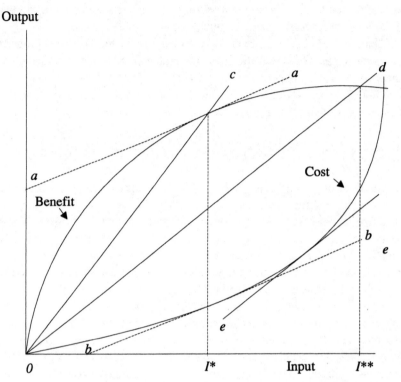

Figure 4.1   An exposition of the misallocation arising from free access
to a common property resource

In the figure, the benefit and cost functions are drawn to show diminishing marginal benefit and increasing marginal cost from applying inputs to a common property resource. The socially efficient outcome is to use an input level of I^*, at which marginal costs and benefits are equal, as shown by the equality of the slopes of the lines aa and bb. In fact free competitive access to the common property resource will lead to an input level at which marginal cost equals average product, which occurs at the input level I^{**}. At this point the average product, given by the slope of Od, equals the marginal cost, given by the slope of ee. Average product is the appropriate measure of the return to input, as it is reasonable to assume that in common property resource situations each unit of input applied to the resource will produce an amount of output equal to the total output divided by the total number of units of input applied.

In other words, there is no distinction between units of the input in terms of their ability to produce output: no distinction can be made between 'earlier' and 'later' units. Thus in a fishery it is assumed that each of n boats will catch one n-th of the total catch: on common grazing land, it is reasonable to expect that all animals will consume equal amounts of the available food.

Clearly this pattern of inputs leads to overuse of the common property resource in the sense that the input is applied beyond the level at which marginal cost and benefit are equal ($I^{**}>I^*$). This is clearly a necessary condition for Pareto efficiency and, under the conditions of increasing marginal cost and diminishing marginal benefit, it is also sufficient.

CORRECTION OF COMMON PROPERTY PROBLEMS

There are three policies commonly used for restoring efficiency in such cases. The first is to assign well-defined property rights in the common property resource. The origins of this approach are found in the work of Coase (1960). Two examples of assigning property rights in this way are the enclosure of common grazing land in Britain in the eighteenth century and of public grazing lands in the US in this century. A more recent and more topical illustration of this approach, which is explained here, is the unitization of oil fields.

If an oilfield covers a large area, several different oil companies may have exploration and development rights on the land over that field. The companies discover the oil and produce from the same pool. Clearly there is a common property resource problem, as the more oil that is produced by one firm, the less there is left for the others. Hence every firm has an incentive to extract as much oil as it can as quickly as possible, before the other firms remove it. Aware of the inefficiency of such a situation, the US has passed a law which requires that all firms in this situation form a joint operating company, operate the field as a single entity and share the proceeds among them. This 'unitization' (McDonald, 1971) eliminates the inter-firm competition that leads to the inefficiently rapid depletion of the oil field and, in effect, establishes a single shared property right where previously there was no well-defined property right.

When exclusive property rights are assigned where they did not previously exist, there is a distributional impact which is typically perceived as negative, accompanied by the creation of an incentive structure that may lead to efficient use of the common property resource. Whether or not it leads to efficiency depends on the degree of competition in the market for the goods produced by the use of the common property resource. The danger here is that by giving one individual or group exclusive property rights in a common property resource one may create a monopoly if that resource provides the only way of producing an important output. It is possible that the exploitation of such a monopoly could be legally restricted by regulation, though there are few practical examples of this. Such a policy has nevertheless the considerable advantage of simplicity, which may make it attractive in many developing countries where administratively simple solutions are rare. This approach clearly does not come within the general rubric of the Polluter-Pays Principle. It does not depend on identifying a polluter, nor on making the polluter or anyone else pay for the externality. It is an approach that works via property rights and the incentives that they establish.

The general approach of dealing with external effects by the introduction of property rights, and then relying on market-generated incentives, has been criticized by Arrow (1979). He argues that this is vulnerable to a 'free-rider' problem. Consider as an illustration of his point a rather different problem.

A factory pollutes the air in its neighborhood, harming nearby residents. The Coasian solution is to assign property rights. In principle it does not matter to which of the parties they are assigned. Assume that they are assigned to the factory, which now has a right to pollute the air. Residents must buy these rights from the factory if they want freedom from pollution. Arrow's argument is that the process of the residents clubbing together to make an offer to the factory will be vulnerable to a free-rider problem, in that any given resident will have an incentive to understate to the group his or her true willingness to contribute to a fund to 'buy out' the factory's pollution rights. The typical resident will hope that the efforts and expenditures of others will prevail. Of course, if all behave like this, then the offer made to the factory will not reflect the true interest of the residents in reducing pollution, and the outcome will not be efficient. At a meta level, the argument is that the act of bargaining about property rights and externalities is a common property resource. While Arrow's criticism of the Coasian approach seems valid in general, it does not seem applicable in the case of assignment of property rights for a common property resource. In this case, there is no bargaining problem in which the free-rider phenomenon can arise.

The second widely recommended approach to the problem of common property resources is to levy a tax on the use of the resource. It can be shown that the appropriate Pigovian tax on the application of inputs to the exploitation of the resource will restore efficiency (Dasgupta and Heal, 1979, Chap. 3), though the issue of how the proceeds of these taxes are to be used in a non-distortionary manner has rarely been addressed. Here an element of the Polluter-Pays Principle may be recognizable. To the extent that each user can be thought of as inflicting generalized 'pollution' on the other users, the Pigovian tax could be construed as an attempt to 'make the polluter pay'. However the fact remains that in the usual sense of the word, there is no pollution here, nor any polluter. If political pressure is used to promote the

Polluter-Pays Principle, then its application to common property problems could be dangerous and provoke a backlash. Users of common property resources, the use of which needs to be curtailed in the interests of efficiency, will not think of themselves as polluters who have to be punished by making restitution to the community. They will be more amenable to an approach which explains the need for Pigovian taxes in terms of conservation in their long-term interest.

A third approach to controlling the use of common property resources to attain efficiency is through permits. There is a general economic presumption in favour of regulation by prices (taxes and subsidies) rather than by quantity, although under specific conditions of uncertainty about the cost and benefit functions associated with use of the common property resource, one can establish a case for quantitative regulation (Weitzman, 1974; - Dasgupta and Heal, 1979, Chap. 13). This case rests on the fact that the level of use of common property resource is fully predictable with a regulatory approach, whereas it is not if one uses prices or property rights as a tool for reaching efficiency. When there are possible strong non-linearities in the cost or benefit functions associated with the use of the resource, this predictability may be of great value because it reduces the risk of a catastrophe.

Tradable permits for the use of a common property resource may combine the advantages of both the quantitative and the market approaches and have been widely advocated (Baumol and Oates, 1988). With tradable permits, the level of use of the resource can be predicted exactly, assuming that compliance can be assured by requiring permits in order to use the resource. Ensuring that the level of use is below a particular level may be important if there are thought to be threshold effects in the response of the resource to exploitation. Such effects can occur, for example, in a fish population when there is a critical stock level such that if the population falls below this level, survival cannot be guaranteed. At the same time, tradable permits are consistent with economic efficiency by ensuring that the burden of adjustment of use levels falls on those for whom the adjustment costs are lowest. There is of course a danger here that if the users of the resource are individuals or families, then the need to purchase permits will shift the burden of adjusting use patterns on to the poorest who can least afford to pay. This issue is reviewed in this volume by Parikh (Chap. 5) and Dommen (Chap. 1). The negative distributional effects of requiring the purchase of permits could be offset by distributing them initially in a way that respects historical use patterns. The introduction of such permits is in principle consistent with the Polluter-Pays Principle, as it requires the user of a common property resource (the 'polluter') to pay to purchase the right to use the resource (to 'pollute'). However, the fact remains that there need be no pollution in the usual sense, so that some semantic flexibility is needed to accommodate this use of 'pollution' to the Polluter-Pays Principle.

All these approaches are shown in Figure 4.1. Taxing the input, to bring its cost from the slope of *bb* to that of *0c*, would ensure efficiency. So would taxing the output to bring the marginal return down from the slope of *0c* to that of *aa*. The use of taxes in either of these ways corresponds to the use of Pigovian taxes. If a single property right were assigned and the common property resource were run by a monopoly that took both input and output prices as given, then the monopolist would choose an input level *I**, as this level maximizes the difference between costs and benefits. Quantitative regulation would of course involve issuing permits to use an amount of input up to the level *I**.

Chichilnisky (1991) illustrates an interesting new approach to the establishment of property rights as a means of internalizing external effects associated with common property resources. It is widely recognized that the existence of tropical rain forests in developing countries, which are common property resources in those countries, has benefits for other countries.

Two mechanisms at least are at work here. The first is the role of tropical forests in converting carbon dioxide into oxygen and biomass, thus helping to rectify the growing concentration of carbon dioxide in the atmosphere and to mitigate harmful effects of climate change (Heal, 1989, 1991). The second mechanism is the role of tropical rain forests as reservoirs of biodiversity. Biodiversity has value for several reasons, one of which is that the organisms found in tropical forests have often been valuable in deriving new pharmaceuticals. For instance, the organisms for several drugs being studied for their capacity to inhibit cancers were found in tropical rain forests. Merck, the pharmaceutical company, recently concluded an agreement with Costa Rica which gives Merck the right to search for potentially useful organisms in the Costa Rican forests. Merck will pay royalties to Costa Rica for drugs developed from organisms found in its forests. By this agreement, Costa Rica is in effect being given a property right in commercial products developed from its common property resources. This is analogous to the property rights conveyed by ownership of a patent (for a more detailed analysis of this case see Chichilnisky, 1991).

COMMON PROPERTY RESOURCES AND INTERNATIONAL TRADE

Recent research (Chichilnisky, 1991) suggests that the legal regime surrounding common property resources is an important determinant of international trade patterns. Suppose that common property resources are used as inputs in the production of goods that are traded internationally. Water resources (used in agricultural production), the atmosphere (used as a sink) and many other common property resources satisfy this condition.

Suppose further that property right regimes differ between countries, particularly with respect to the use of common property resources, but that in all other respects (i.e. endowments, technologies, personal preferences) countries are identical. Differences in property rights are reflected in differences in the cash cost of using common property resources, and therefore in the supply conditions of goods produced from common property resources. Chichilnisky (1991) analyses international trade patterns that arise under such circumstances, and proves that the differences in property right regimes can lead to a spurious appearance of comparative advantage. She shows that the country with the less well-defined property rights in the common property resources will have a supply function for the good produced from them that is more elastic with respect to price, and that as a consequence this country will export the good intensive in the common property resource at an equilibrium pattern of international trade. To quote Chichilnisky (1991): 'differences in property right systems may provide a basis for international trade, with the country with weak property rights exporting the goods which use intensively the common property resource. The outcome can be an inefficient allocation worldwide.' Trade based on differences in the systems of property rights for common property resources will not lead to an efficient international division of labour. Indeed, Chichilnisky (1991) argues that developing countries typically have less well-developed property rights in common property resources than do industrial countries, as the latter have better developed legal systems and so have in place the infrastructure for defining and monitoring property rights. Hence developing countries will typically tend to export goods that are intensive in the use of common property resources, such as water resources, grazing lands, the atmosphere, etc. Differences in property rights systems are a possible explanation for the concentration of developing countries in the export of agricultural products and of products that are heavily polluting. Chichilnisky's analysis also suggests that such concentration is disadvantageous to developing countries.

These results imply that the treatment of common property resources is important not only for of achieving an efficient use of resources domestically, but also for establishing a beneficial relationship with the international market.

5. THE POLLUTER-PAYS AND USER-PAYS PRINCIPLES FOR DEVELOPING COUNTRIES: MERITS, DRAWBACKS AND FEASIBILITY

Kirit S. Parikh

INTRODUCTION

The Polluter-Pays Principle (PPP), developed to manage environmental pollution, and the User-Pays Principle (UPP) to manage exhaustible natural resources efficiently, are fundamentally the same. Essentially, pollution can be looked upon as the use of environmental carrying capacity or of environmental quality. The idea behind these two principles is to internalize the economic costs of the external effects of production, consumption and disposal. Among these costs are the costs of controlling effluents and cleaning up the environment, and the costs borne by society for damage due to the residual pollution which is within the permissible limits, as well as costs imposed on others due to loss of options.

Usually, the environmental costs are beyond the decision-making process of economic agents. When they are fully internalized, the market mechanism can be expected to help limit the use of exhaustible resources to levels consistent with sustainable development, induce development and adoption of resource conservation methods and pollution abatement techniques, and to avoid distortions in investment allocations and trade patterns. These results are achieved, however, only when the following conditions, as they relate to a producer, are fulfilled.

- perfect competition in the product market;
- increasing production costs;
- increasing costs of pollution abatement; and
- negligible monitoring costs.

If the above conditions are met, a firm governed by PPP pays the long-run marginal social cost for the pollution it creates. The firm then will take measures to abate the pollution so that the marginal cost of abatement equals the long-run marginal social cost; in the long run a cost-effective abatement will occur.

The two main approaches to environmental policies are either command and control (C and C) or market based. Under C and C policies, firms are required to maintain their effluents within prescribed limits which are set in the light of the best available technology, and to meet certain efficiency standards by a given date. The policies require that the regulators are aware of the best available technology or attainable standards. Even if every firm meets the effluent discharge standard, the quality of water or air may continue to worsen as the number of firms increases.

PPP can be better appreciated by looking at alternative approaches to environmental policies.

The market-friendly approaches include pollution charges, tradable pollution permits, subsidies as incentives for pollution abatement, and input charges or output taxes. A pollution charge induces a firm to curtail its pollution to the level where the marginal cost of abatement equals the charge. If the charge is appropriate, firms will be induced to adopt the best available abatement technology, but they would still have to pay the charge on the residual pollution (which they would not do under a C and C policy).

It is sometimes argued that though the residual pollution causes damage, it is compensated by gains to society (for example, through employment generation). The firms, therefore, need not pay for residual damage. The OECD (1975) statement on PPP does not consider payments for residual damage obligatory nor contrary to PPP. When compensation for residual damage is required, PPP is called the extended PPP (Pezzey, 1988).

Setting a pollution charge at a rate that leads to an optimal pollution level requires considerable information (though less than that required by C and C policies). One needs to determine the social cost of the pollution function and also the long-run marginal cost of abatement in order to equate it with the long-run marginal social cost. The same problem occurs with pollution charges as with the C and C policy in that an ambient air quality cannot be ensured since a growing number of firms can increase total pollution beyond the desired level.

Tradable permits do contain the total pollution to an acceptable level. Initially, these permits can be either auctioned or allocated. When auctioned, they correspond to the extended PPP as the firms pay for all the residual pollution as well as for their abatement measures. (The proceeds of the auction should be distributed equally to all members of society.) When they are allocated to firms free of charge, they conform to the standard PPP where firms pay only for their abatement measures and not for the residual pollution. This initial allotment need not correspond to the optimal distribution, as any deviation from it will be corrected by trade in such rights. But if firms are allocated rights in excess of their final level of pollution, they gain extra income.

At the country level a case can be made for not charging firms for residual pollution, but not at the international level where the extended PPP should be applied. Just as in the national case, the proceeds of an international auction should be distributed equally to all people on earth.

Input charges and output taxes do not strictly correspond to PPP as they do not provide incentives for optimal abatement. They are, however, easy to administer.

The use of PPP and UPP to manage resources and environment should be attractive to governments of market economies. Yet their use in developing countries needs to be examined for several reasons. Many people, particularly the poor, are on the periphery of the market economy and their behaviour is only marginally affected by it. The most pressing environmental problems in developing countries are degradation of land, deforestation, urban congestion, insanitary living conditions in urban slums, and severe air pollution particularly in urban areas, caused by millions of small producers and consumers. While behaviour may be changed most easily through market mechanisms, it may be difficult, given the large number of actors, to find fiscal measures to internalize the externalities which can be enforced at a reasonable cost. Also, the use of fiscal measures can have a regressive effect on the poor, whose livelihood depends on common property resources for their basic needs of food, fuel and fodder. If the environmental cost of the use of those resources were internalized, the poor would suffer deprivation, unless they received compensatory subsidies. The consequent increase in the market value of the use of the resources provides incentives for the more powerful to appropriate them. The property rights are often not clearly defined and even when they are there may be no mechanisms for equitable access and use.

In this chapter, we explore the possibilities and the usefulness of PPP and UPP for developing countries.

MANAGING MAJOR ENVIRONMENTAL PROBLEMS USING PPP

In this section, we examine whether PPP can be used effectively to deal with a number of problems.

Air Pollution in Urban Areas: Industrial, Vehicular and Domestic missions

While the sources of air pollution in many developing countries are similar to those in developed countries, several characteristics of developing countries may make it more difficult to apply PPP.

The industrial sector in an urban area in a developing country usually has many medium, small and tiny (or informal) enterprises which often dominate industrial production in terms of value added. These units are dispersed throughout the city, but are often concentrated in congested slums. They use a vast variety of techniques and equipment of different vintages. As long as a machine is working, it is not discarded for someone is always willing to operate it at a still lower implicit wage rate.

Many of the small- and medium-scale enterprises (SMEs) operate in highly competitive markets and any addition to their costs, if not also imposed on their competitors, would seriously undermine their viability.

Using PPP in such an environment creates difficulties. A pollution charge necessitates monitoring the emissions from many small enterprises. Although a fuel tax may be easier to impose, its effectiveness in reducing pollution efficiently is questionable. For example, if coal is taxed, some people may switch to traditional fuels such as wood, which may be even more polluting. Many SMEs are not able to install economically efficient abatement equipment because they are unable to obtain loans. They may lose competitiveness to larger firms with better access to credit and abatement technology. Also, abatement technologies could have economies of scale which could adversely affect SME competitiveness. Tiny household enterprises which have no alternatives may have to close down. Welfare would be worsened. Exempting SMEs from pollution charges may not be an option: 'smallness' is often faked by Indian industries to get incentives given to small enterprises. One can expect that it would also be faked to avoid pollution charges.

Industrial emissions

Conversely, obstacles to the effectiveness of PPP policies in developing countries may be hindered by the dominance of a few large industrial firms. For example, in India in 1987-88, in 99 product groups out of 156, the top four firms had a market share exceeding 60 per cent (CMIE, 1989). Firms with monopoly power can pass on a PPP-based pollution charge to their consumers whose response will not result in socially optimal abatement. Such firms can also exercise market power, both in the initial auction of emission permits and in subsequent trading. They may corner emission permits to prevent the entry and growth of competing firms. In these situations, it may be better to use a mix of C and C and PPP policies.

Vehicular emissions

Emissions from motor vehicles are a major source of urban air pollution in cities of developing countries. Poorly maintained old cars and trucks, and scooters and motorcycles, crawl slowly on these cities' congested roads.

A direct pollution tax would be difficult to impose on these kinds of vehicles. Even if such a tax could be collected, its incentive effect in reducing pollution would be minimal. Vehicle owners may have no alternative. A fuel tax for small truck firms operating one or two old vehicles may face the same loss of competitiveness as discussed in the previous section. A tax on new vehicles commensurate with the pollution they cause is feasible but unless there is some degree of competition, the tax may simply be passed on to the consumer with no improvement in emissions. In many developing countries competition is indeed limited. Even if a tax is effective for new vehicles, the pace at which the old stock is replaced is likely to be slow. A purchase tax or an annual tax is not enough of an incentive for the operator to use the vehicle less frequently.

Domestic emissions

Household fuel is an important source of environmental pollution in developing countries. Dirty fuels (wood, dung-cakes, etc.) in poorly ventilated kitchens and in congested urban slums cause severe pollution and adversely affect health, particularly of women and children. Taxing dirty fuels according to PPP would be regressive. The energy consumption of the urban poor has hardly any discretionary element in it. Dirty fuels are used either because they are the only ones accessible or because they are comparatively cheap; poor households would rather tolerate this situation than pay more for a cleaner fuel. A tax on dirty fuels would not improve the efficiency of use, but only make the poor, poorer. It makes sense only if an alternative fuel is provided at a reasonable cost.

Land Degradation due to Agricultural Use

Land degradation due to agricultural use results mainly from chemical fertilizers, pesticides and irrigation. We consider the case of fertilizers as it is the most important of these inputs.

Use of fertilizer leads to chemical pollution of the soil due to residual fertilizer; it pollutes both surface run-off as well as groundwater. PPP would charge farmers for the water pollution they cause (leaving aside the deterioration of their own land due to chemical residuals). Even if the value of water pollution is known, it is difficult to measure the pollution and to allocate responsibility among farmers.

Water quality would have to be measured to determine the amount of pollution. It varies significantly over the year. The pattern of run-off and recharge depends on rainfall and weather, and farmers use fertilizers only at intervals; so water quality would need to be measured frequently. Naturally the costs of such measurements would be high and the administrative feasibility of reliable measurement low.

Even though reliable and cost-effective measurement of water quality (e.g. inexpensive automatic recording devices) is possible, allocating responsibility among individual farmers is an extremely difficult problem because farm holdings are small and fragmented. For example, in India the average farm size is 1.26 ha and the average number of fragments exceeds four (NSSO, 1990). Even in a micro-watershed, the point where water quality is measured may be fed by hundreds of plots belonging to different farmers growing different crops, using different quantities and types of fertilizer and following different cultivation practices. Their contributions to water pollution are thus different. Moreover, the pollution from subsurface flows depends upon how aquifers are connected; the pollution may even originate from outside the watershed (see Fig. 5.1). A consistent application of PPP that will induce the farmers to reduce pollution efficiently in social terms is not possible in these circumstances.

However, if all the pollution is due to fertilizer residues, one may ask why not levy a tax on fertilizer? Could this be done in a way that is consistent with PPP? Unfortunately there is not a one-to-one correspondence between the application of fertilizer and the resulting pollution. Fertilizer could be carefully applied so as to reduce residues. If this is done, a tax on fertilizer is not as efficient as a tax on pollution (Figure 5.2).

A tax on fertilizer would definitely reduce its use, but might not lead to appropriate adoption of pollution-reducing techniques. Nonetheless, a tax on fertilizer is easy to collect. Investment subsidies could be given to farmers who install pollution-reducing equipment (e.g. drip irrigation).

Degradation of Common Property Resources

In many poor developing countries with scarce land, degradation of the village commons, deforestation, overfishing from the village pond or overexploitation of groundwater resources create environmental problems that adversely affect

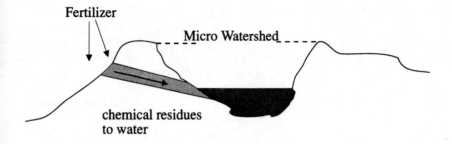

Figure 5.1: Subsurface pollution from outside the watershed.

the population, particularly the poor for whom those resources are especially important. The landless need to gather twigs, lops and tops for fuel and to graze their animals on the village commons. With a growing population, the regenerative productivity of the land is soon exceeded by demand and the land deteriorates. Can PPP or UPP be used to manage it?

A common property pasture is given here as an example; the arguments apply to other common property resources as well. Assume that the policy objective is to limit grazing. Individuals could be given quotas in 'animal hours'. This C and C system would keep the pasture productive. Or, a charge could be imposed on grazing land by auctioning grazing rights, so that the demand for grazing would equal the sustainable supply. The proceeds of such a sale of rights could be distributed equitably to all concerned. This arrangement would be consistent with UPP but may create some problems in developing countries, e.g. the auction may be dominated by wealthy landholders, or the arrangement may deprive the poor of options to earn an income in the future. The poor do not have easy access to credit and if they are obliged to pay for fodder would not be able to keep animals. They thus lose the opportunity to employ their own labour in looking after animals. It would be better to allocate the grazing rights equitably at the outset and allow trade thereafter.

The situation becomes more complex because village commons often have multiple products and uses: e.g. the common provides fodder, it is a source of fuel, artisans and craftsmen get their raw materials from local woods (they need to have the right species of trees for this purpose), etc. In the absence of an effective system, marketization through UPP would hurt some of the poor and would create more incentives for others to appropriate the resources.

Yield

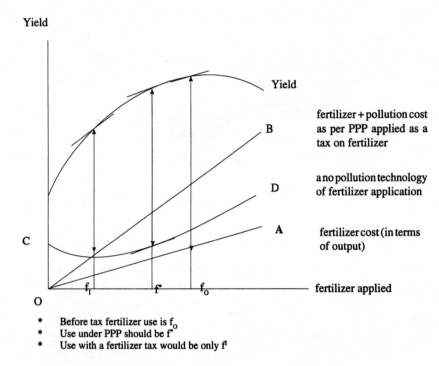

* Before tax fertilizer use is f_o
* Use under PPP should be f^*
* Use with a fertilizer tax would be only f^1

Figure 5.2. Taxing fertilizer is not fully consistent with PPP.

A fair initial allocation of tradable/leasable user rights is consistent with UPP and leads efficiently to sustainable use of the common property although new institutional arrangements may be required to achieve this end.

Environmental Problems due to Irrigation

The problems of salination, waterlogging and changes in groundwater levels, are in some ways similar to the problems of common property resources.

The many small cultivators make the monitoring of actual water use difficult. The lack of one-to-one correspondence between the quantity of water used and the resulting environmental consequences create for PPP the same difficulties as does fertilizer. However, unlike the use of a common property pasture or woodland, the rate of extraction of groundwater is difficult to measure, monitor and control, because it is extracted by farmers from their own fields and wells. Thus it is not easy to keep extraction within allocated rights.

PPP AND NON-MARKET CONSIDERATIONS IN THE ECONOMIC DECISIONS OF THE POOR

The importance of non-market considerations in the economic decisions of the poor also raise questions concerning the use of PPP-based policies which rely mainly on the market mechanism.

Markets are not well developed, nor does everyone have equal access to them. A small farmer with a meagre surplus living in a remote area may not be connected by a good road to a market which may render his transaction costs prohibitive. Traders acquire monopoly power under such conditions. Growing one's own food in such a situation increases food security for those who are on the margin of survival. The payoff function is highly asymmetric for a small and marginal farmer. When the crop is larger than usual, he does well, but when it fails he may starve. If he has also incurred debts to buy inputs such as fertilizers, which would be more expensive with a PPP-based tax, his vulnerability increases. He may have to borrow money at a high interest rate (because of the poor functioning of credit markets) or may have to sell his assets (bullocks, land, etc.) and his earning ability will suffer. A fertilizer tax should be accompanied by extended credit opportunities for small farmers, or by a crop insurance scheme although these are difficult to implement in a self-financing way.

PPP, INTERNATIONAL NEGOTIATIONS AND TRADE

The use of the extended PPP at the international level is crucial for dealing with the global commons. C and C policies involve avoidable costs. A system of equitably allocated tradable (leasable) emission quotas and a set of futures markets for them have much to recommend them. Without such a system many less developed countries would not be able to participate in international agreements. For example, exempting less developed countries for a few years from CO_2 emission limits can lead to some undesirable outcomes: the less developed countries will not have any incentive to reduce their emissions; polluting industries from developed countries will have an incentive to move to less developed countries; and the less developed countries might exhaust their future margin and incur emission constraints. Instituting leasable emission quotas will encourage less developed countries to adopt efficient technologies. Tradable quotas will stimulate trade in technology and the developing countries will be in a better position to purchase new technology at favourable prices.

Under a C and C agreement such as the Montreal Protocol on chlorofluorocarbons, a developing country is required to lower emissions and has no choice but to purchase whatever abatement technology is available; if there is a monopoly supplier a monopoly price will be extracted. Under PPP-based tradable emissions quotas, the developing country is not required to purchase the technology and thus obtain it at a better price. Can a developing country accept PPP policies at an international level while it finds it difficult to follow them domestically? The answer should be yes. PPP recognizes that different standards may be appropriate in different situations. It permits subsidies and income support to meet specific social objectives. A developing country may want to forfeit some efficiency gains resulting from PPP policies for social objectives. It may also find that the efficiency gains are at times more than offset by implementation costs. Domestically it may, therefore, adopt a mix of C and C and PPP policies.

CONCLUSIONS

In conclusion, we summarize the major points of thischapter:

1. By internalizing the externalities of environmental damage and resource depletion, the Polluter-Pays Principle (PPP) and the User-Pays Principle (UPP) provide a framework for policies that can be economically efficient. If such policies can work through the market mechanism, they would be incentive-compatible and likely to be successful.

2. The cases discussed identify two main difficulties in applying PPP in developing countries. The large number of small polluters create nearly insurmountable problems for measurement and monitoring. The lack of well-functioning insurance and credit markets and of equal access to credit for both big and small agents may deny the small agents the possibilities to respond rationally to PPP-based policies.

3. What these examples have also shown is that for the most important environmental problems of developing countries, PPP-based policies are likely to cause distress to the poorer segments of society. In a sense this should have been foreseen: poverty itself is a cause of pollution and much environmental stress in developing countries is a consequence of the constraints facing the poor who have to live off the natural resources available to them. Any attempt to make them more expensive without increasing the incomes of the poor is bound to make them worse off.

4. We have seen that administration of PPP-based policies in developing countries is more difficult than in developed countries because of the large number of pollution sources. Yet the same difficulties of measurement and monitoring also apply to command and control policies. Thus, though the application of PPP may be difficult in many cases, it may not be more difficult than C and C policies.

5. In their basic form, some PPP policies are not practical for developing countries. Yet the PPP approach in environmental policy design has much to be said for it. Together with appropriate supplementary measures, such as easier access to credit, crop insurance schemes, and compensatory income transfers to the poor, PPP and UPP are attractive principles for policy design.

6. Village communities in developing countries are likely to be dominated by only a few households. In societies with an unequal distribution of power, it is important to use the extended PPP to manage the village commons. To be fair the initial allocation of user rights should be equal per capita. This is also important for the urban industrial sectors in developing countries where a few large firms dominate most sectors.

7. Similarly, because of the inequality among countries, in international negotiations and with respect to the global commons, developing countries are well advised to insist on using the extended PPP. The cost of preserving the global commons is high and the developing countries should not have to pay more than their share. A system of tradable (better still, only leasable) emission quotas given to all countries based on some accepted principle of social justice and equity will be most desirable. It will be consistent with PPP and would not have to be set but the price of quotas would be determined by trade. Any desired ambient quality can be attained at minimum cost. Individual countries remain free to select their own environmental priorities and their own domestic policies to attain their environmental objectives. They will also have incentives for abatement and conservation as their quotas are likely to have high opportunity costs. Tradable quotas will stimulate trade in technology at better prices than under C and C policies.

6. APPLICATION OF THE POLLUTER-PAYS PRINCIPLE IN LATIN AMERICA

GONZALO BIGGS[1]

> Water is the greatest element of nutrition ... but is easily polluted. You cannot poison the soil, or the sun or the air ... but all these things may very likely happen in regard to water, but which must therefore be protected by law ... If anyone intentionally spoils the water of another ... let him not only pay damages, but purify the stream or cistern which contains the water ...
>
> (Plato)[2]

BACKGROUND

The ultimate purpose of environmental management and policy should be to improve the quality of life and ensure the long-term sustainability of the renewable natural resources of a country. Various regulatory or economic instruments may be employed to achieve these purposes, whose effectiveness will depend on the institutional structure or development level of the country or region.

Based on this premiss, this essay examines the feasibility or usefulness of applying, among such instruments, the Polluter-Pays Principle (PPP) or its relative the User-Pays Principle (UPP) in Latin America and the Caribbean.[3] The emphasis of this analysis is on PPP as an incentive for the payment of pollution prevention or control costs by the corresponding economic agent rather than through higher charges or levies.

Irrespective of the fact that the levels of industrial pollution are considerably higher in OECD countries as compared with Latin American countries, PPP would have been, or is perceived as having been, successful in preventing or reducing the effects of pollution in the former countries. A presumption exists then that similar benefits would result from the application of these two principles in Latin America. This essay is a preliminary analysis of a very complex subject which does not intend to confirm or rebut the above presumptions but only to highlight some factors that should be taken into consideration in the eventual application of PPP in Latin America. It is noted also that there are strong supporters and opponents of PPP in Latin America; the supporters see it as an additional reflection of the consolidation of a market economy in this region, while the opponents reject its implication that tolerable levels of pollution by selected economic agents may be condoned or admitted or that regulatory measures should be discarded.

This analysis includes a reference to: the economic impact that could be expected from the application of PPP in Latin America; this region's institutional, legal and policy framework; the operational issues; and those other policy instruments from which PPP should be distinguished. Emphasis is given to the differences between the environmental problems of OECD and Latin American countries, the importance of national accounts in the calculation of environmental degradation, the relation of PPP to technology transfer, the role of transnational corporations, the national treatment principle and President Bush's Enterprise for the Americas Initiative. Two annexes are attached to this chapter which include references to the legislation (Annex A) and water resources (Annex B) of Latin America.

INTERNATIONAL IMPACT

The specific economic impact which the operation of the PPP has already had on the export prices of manufactured goods of OECD countries is not, to our knowledge, available. However, from various sources it has been estimated that the costs of pollution control in some industrialized countries may be as high as 3 per cent of their GDPs.[4] Although this figure does not include the specific costs represented by the application of PPP in OECD countries, it indirectly confirms its economic significance. Whatever their amount, however, it must be assumed that those pollution costs have been reflected in those prices as from the date PPP became operative. Hence, they would have already been paid by the Latin American and other countries in their merchandise trade with OECD countries. In theory then and without prejudice to its domestic impact, application of PPP could, in this sense, be beneficial to Latin America as it could have the potential of compensating this region's chronic terms of trade deterioration with OECD countries.[5] However, a sudden allocation of environmental costs to the prices of Latin America's manufactures or primary commodities would not be feasible as it could either render them totally uncompetitive or cause a major disruption to international trade. Consequently, prior to the application of PPP in Latin America, and in order to prevent trade disruptions, an analysis of the following data would appear to be essential: (i) the impact which PPP has had in the international prices of OECD manufactured goods since its date of application; and (ii) the impact which PPP would have on the domestic and export prices of manufactures and primary commodities in Latin America.

INSTITUTIONAL FRAMEWORK

Institutions or principles reflect a society's idiosyncrasies and economic development levels and therefore may not always be adapted efficiently by other societies.

In Latin America, institutions and ideologies have traditionally been incorporated from other countries or regions but the overall result of these experiences may be described as mixed at best. Thus, European or North American political constitutions or electoral laws have at times been reproduced almost verbatim in other less developed countries but have rarely operated as effectively as their Northern Hemisphere counterparts. These failures may be attributed to what in modern terminology is generically referred to as the issue of 'governance', or lack thereof. Thus, in what refers to environmental policy, the application of PPP should be integrated within the broader and ongoing process of capacity building which has resulted from UNCED (1992b). The following paragraphs list some of the factors considered essential for this analysis.

IMPLEMENTATION

There are no mechanisms for coordinating or implementing regional environmental policies in Latin America and the Caribbean which can be compared with those established for its members by the OECD Convention of 1960[6] or by the proposed European Environment Agency of the EC. Neither the Organization of American States, the Inter-American Development Bank, nor any other regional or subregional institution of the Latin American or Caribbean regions, have the powers or the mandate to adopt binding decisions or recommendations on matters related to environmental policies or principles.[7] Consequently, in the absence of such mechanisms or powers, the adoption or implementation of such policies or principles can only be carried out by each individual country on a case-by-case basis. This, of course, raises major practical problems for the adoption of PPP in the Latin American region as a whole; it also supports the view that its applicability can only be considered in specific countries.

LEGISLATION

Environmental legislation is an important instrument for the application of environmental policy. However, in Latin America, with few exceptions, this legislation is exclusively sectoral, incidental or dispersed in heterogenous statutes with sometimes contradictory objectives (see Brañes, 1991). In addition, pollution problems are sanctioned with administrative or even criminal penalties which, in practice, are rarely imposed.[8] Moreover, notwithstanding its importance, the institutional framework required for the enforcement of environmental policies or regulations is, in most cases, non-existent. A discouraging precedent for the application of PPP and UPP are also the high percentages of tax evasion and of arrearages in the payment of tariffs for basic services and utilities which in some countries can exceed 50 per cent.

Without prejudice to the above, PPP has been included in the water management legislation of some Latin American countries, as is indicated in Annex A of this chapter.

NEED FOR COMPREHENSIVE POLICIES

The application of PPP in OECD countries reflects a degree of institutional sophistication not yet achieved in Latin America and made more difficult by this region's current transition to an open market economy. This does not mean to say that the application of PPP is not feasible or should not be adopted, but only that considerable time may still be needed before this principle can be applied effectively. One major obstacle is, precisely, the mistaken notion that transition to a market economy must give priority to unrestricted economic growth without consideration to its effects on the natural environment.

The above is compounded by the detrimental consequences brought to the natural environment of the region by the external debt crisis of the 1980s. This crisis, together with the structural adjustment policies applied thereafter, drastically reduced investments and budget allocations for non-productive activities, particularly for the social sectors. The pressure to restore economic growth and at the same time service the external debt received exclusive priority, and measures to protect the environment, including capacity building and support of environmental protection agencies and institutions, were continually postponed. Worse still, policies were adopted which were clearly detrimental to the environment; such was the case with those policies which maximized the export of primary commodities through tax incentives or credit subsidies with little or no consideration of their effects on the natural environment. A case in point were those policies which expanded the agricultural frontier into the Amazon region or the Central American natural forests and wetlands with harmful consequences to the latter.

These major obstacles will only be overcome when governments at their highest levels recognize that environmental considerations must be fully incorporated into their economic policies and decisions. The adoption, therefore, of a comprehensive policy of sustainable development endorsed at the cabinet level, the enactment of appropriate legislation, the reinforcement of institutions and appointment of competent technical staff to enforce those policies are essential prerequisites for executing measures of environmental protection, including the adoption and application of PPP.[9] Consequently, the eventual adoption of PPP cannot derive from isolated measures but must be an integral component of comprehensive sustainable development policies.

A subsequent challenge in this process would be the harmonization of those policies, and of PPP at the regional and, ultimately, global levels.

PROCEDURES

How can the above objectives be achieved?

Without prejudice to the impulse which the decisions adopted by the participating governments at the Rio Summit in June 1992 will give to sustainable development, an effective method for achieving these objectives could be the structural adjustment loans of international financial institutions. However, until now these institutions have not given environmental policies the priority they require in Latin American countries. This should change very quickly though, particularly as a result of the decisions taken in Rio by UNCED. Hence, when appropriate policies are adopted, governments will be able to define the sphere of application of PPP. For these purposes, each country or sectoral activity may require a different methodology or policy strategy for whose adoption the experience of OECD countries should be most helpful. Indeed, at the appropriate time, the technical cooperation of the OECD could be instrumental for the successful application and implementation of the PPP in Latin America.

OPERATIONAL ISSUES

Operatively, the following major questions would have to be addressed by the Latin American Governments:

- to what industries or activities could the principle be first applied?
- to what type of pollution would the principle apply?

- under what criteria would the charges be calculated?
- what would be the schedule for the enforcement of the principle?
- what standards would apply for the operations or activities of state agencies and how would they be enforced?
- would private individuals have legal standing to enforce compliance with PPP?
- who would administer the resources generated by the pollution charges and what would be the destiny of the corresponding funds?
- who would ultimately bear the pollution costs? the consumer? the producre? the government? or, all of them?
- would subsidies be maintained during the transition period? If so, with what criteria?

Each of the above questions involve major issues which would have to be addressed by any government that resolves to adopt PPP but further exploration of them is beyond the scope of this chapter.

OTHER INSTRUMENTS

The adoption of PPP should not convey the impression that pollution is permissible or inevitable or that either the general public or governments are deprived from the exercise of legal remedies or regulatory powers whenever warranted or justified. The perception that the eventual adoption of this principle will be equivalent to a licence to pollute within certain limits, or that it would constitute a waiver from legal responsibilities, is not acceptable. PPP should, therefore, be ancillary or complementary to the existing regulatory instruments.

In this regard, it should be recalled that one of the most successful examples of pollution prevention of recent times (the elimination of the lead content of gasoline in the United States) was effected through legal fiat and not by market mechanisms.

Consequently, PPP should be distinguished from those situations where other remedies or recourses apply and should continue to apply.

Specifically, PPP should be distinguished from:

(a) the exercise by private individuals of those traditional remedies recognized by Latin American law for demanding indemnification for the pecuniary damages caused to life or property by non-contractual involuntary actions or omissions;

(b) the discharge of the strict responsibility of any individual or legal entity, including government agencies, for the damages caused to the environment or third parties, irrespective of culpability and other penalties, through the payment of the corresponding indemnification, as established in the legislation of certain countries;[10]

(c) the government power to demand from foreign investments or new industrial projects the adoption of specifications or technologies for reducing or eliminating the levels of permissible pollution in accordance with previously established standards;

(d) the government power to regulate economic activities and impose whatever measures may be appropriate, including the closing of an industry, in specific cases of contamination.

(e) the enforcement of a country's international responsibility through the payment of appropriate compensation for transboundary environmental damage resulting from industrial or maritime accidents pursuant to international agreements or principles providing for strict liability, compulsory insurance or advanced allocation of financial resources for coverage of partial liability; and

(f) the responsibility of industry for the safety, health and working conditions of its employees and the community in general.

DIFFERENCES FROM OECD COUNTRIES

The environmental problems of Latin America are different from those of OECD countries. These differences are basically socio-economic but also reflect separate geophysical realities. For instance, Latin America possesses some of the world's largest sustainable water resources, but since they are located away from the great urban and industrialized centres they are therefore not affected by the same pollution problems as the Rhine, Danube, or the Great Lakes of North America (see Annex B). Consequently, while in the industrialized North the problems of toxic or hazardous waste disposal have the foremost priority and fully justify the use of PPP, the impact of these problems is not the same in Latin America; indeed, in this region, the problems of extreme poverty, human settlements, urban concentration, deforestation or soil degradation have a higher priority and hence require different solutions from those provided by PPP.

A blatant paradox also is that, while in countries like France or Germany, 100 per cent of the population have access to drinking water and sanitation services, in Latin America 38 per cent, or 147 million out of a population of 383 million in 1985, had no potable water, and 65 per cent, or 250 million people, had no sewerage (Alfaro, 1989, p. 383). For people without these services the issue therefore is not water pollution from industrial activities to which PPP could be applicable, but accessibility to this basic resource. Hence, the subsidization of the supply of potable water or sewerage services for low-income groups in Latin America is justified for reasons which do not exist in France or Germany.

IMPORTANCE OF PRIMARY COMMODITIES

As a region, the Latin American economy continues to depend on the exploitation and export of primary commodities which, in 1990, represented around two-thirds of total exports, including mineral fuels (24.4 per cent).[11] In addition, primary commodities were an important component of its manufactures. Moreover, in 1990, only three countries, Argentina, Brazil and Mexico, accounted for 80.29 per cent of the region's export of manufactures, with Brazil and Mexico together representing 70.05 per cent (United Nations Statistical Office, 1990). The total share of the export of manufactures of the rest of the countries was 19.71 per cent and for some 15 countries manufactures represented less than 1 per cent of their total exports *(ibid)* In addition, manufactures represented less than 1 per cent of the total exports of some 15 countries.

ENVIRONMENTAL DEGRADATION

The Latin American economic dependency on the exploitation of its natural resources, together with its incorporation into an open market economy, will probably exacerbate its environmental problems. This is because of the imperative to maximize the growth of external trade. What is worrisome is that the environmental impact of activities which rely predominantly on the exploitation of natural resources may be less visible but more damaging in the long term to the Latin American countries than is industrial pollution to OECD countries. Such is the situation with soil erosion, the destruction of biodiversity, desertification or the spillover of chemical fertilizers into rivers or oceans. UNEP has characterized the 'degradation of ecosystems, the projected disappearance of some tropical forests' as among the most difficult environmental issues to resolve because they

> are often inconspicuous, are not felt immediately, are difficult to quantify, and like issues of health, education and social benefits, are not easily reducible to the standard cost-benefit equations, methods and objectives that guide countries negotiations and decision-makers, and may often involve forgoing today's tangible economic benefits for tomorrow's intangibles (UNEP, 1984, p.12).

As may be noted, to address the challenges of ecosystem degradation referred to by UNEP, and which are critical to Latin America, PPP would have little applicability.

PRIVATIZATION

The structural adjustment process of the last decade has included, or been followed by, the privatization of large segments of the public sector of many countries. This greater reliance in the private sector has been or is being accompanied by a gradual switch from the use of regulatory policies to the use of economic incentives or disincentives.

PPP would be consistent with this trend and could fill whatever gaps may exist in the regulatory framework. Without prejudice to its limitations (which have been mentioned in this paper), PPP would thus be a useful instrument to provide incentives to the private sector to both prevent and control pollution.

ENVIRONMENTAL DEGRADATION AND INDUSTRIAL POLLUTION

Long-term environmental degradation which results from the overexploitation of natural resources must be distinguished from industrial pollution. To address the first category of problems, a comprehensive policy of sustainable development would include both regulatory and market instruments. According to a recent study (ECLAC, 1991), to achieve this purpose the national accounts should be expanded to include as assets, and not as revenues, the natural resources of the respective countries. This is, of course, a formidable task which may take many years to execute and involve multiple actions, including the preparation of a physical inventory, the assessment of each country's natural resources, and the adjustment of the methodology for the internalization of the environmental costs of production.

The problems of industrial pollution, on the other hand, would be distinct from those of environmental degradation and may be addressed with other measures, including PPP. However, although the methodology may be different, the end result of using the national accounts to reflect the costs of long-term environmental degradation, or PPP to reflect the immediate costs of industrial pollution, should, in the long term, be roughly similar. Indeed, both methods should be compatible and mutually reinforcing, and ultimately reflect the environmental costs of the production of all goods and services. Their international impact would be different, though, as non-fuel primary commodities from Latin America account for 13.9 per cent of world commodities trade, while the export of manufactures from this same region accounts for 1.9 per cent of the world manufactures trade (United Nations Statistical Office, 1990). However, the marginal role of Latin America's manufactures in international trade does not mean that this activity has no domestic importance or that it cannot have detrimental consequences to the natural environment of the countries of the region. Indeed, the opposite is probably true. Consequently, irrespective of its impact on international trade, every industrial activity within the region could be subject to the application of PPP.

CAPITAL ACCOUNTS

Long-term improvement in environmental management can be achieved if countries charge part of their natural resources revenues to capital accounts instead of to income. A study by Repetto (1991) in Indonesia mentions that, if depreciation for oil, forestry and soil assets had been accounted for between 1971 and 1984, that country's GDP would have been reduced from 7.1 per cent to 4 per cent during those years. In other words, according to this study, between 1971 and 1984 Indonesia would have partially consumed its natural assets to the detriment of its future generations. A similar calculation was made by Repetto *et al.* (1991a and b) on the effects of resource depletion in Costa Rica during 1970 and 1989. Although the full accounting of environmental costs to the capital accounts as suggested may not be immediately feasible, Repetto *et al.* raise valid questions as to the manner in which revenues from natural resources have been and are being included in the calculations of the GDP. The significance which such an innovation would have for Latin America justifies that it be given serious consideration.

TECHNOLOGY TRANSFER

A source of concern in the application of PPP is that industries with the greatest technological capacity will better absorb the costs of pollution. This raises problems for Latin American industries because transnational corporations (TNCs) will normally have that technological advantage and a strict application of the PPP may remove from business the least competitive which would be the domestic industries. The interest of developing countries, on the other hand, is that environmentally sound technologies be diffused and not monopolized by a few large corporations. How can this be accomplished without infringing on the foreign investment agreements reached by host governments and TNCs? Or, how can this situation be compatible with the ongoing pressures to grant 20-year intellectual property rights to foreign corporations? These are issues which, like others relating to technology transfer, have not yet been resolved at the global level and which are made more evident by the eventual application of PPP.

TRANSNATIONAL CORPORATIONS

TNCs are important in the application of PPP as they hold a significant stake in the extractive and manufacturing industries of Latin America.

Although major disasters involving TNCs, such as those of Bhopal, India in 1984 or Seveso, Italy in 1976, have not yet occurred in Latin America, their environmental record, particularly in the mining industry, is less than acceptable. The copper tailings contamination of the river Mantaro in Central Peru[12] and of the port of Chañaral in Northern Chile (see Asenjo, 1989, pp. 99-110), and the industrial pollution of the Mexican northern border by foreign 'maquiladoras' (assembly plants), are well-known illustrations of the permissiveness with which foreign investments have operated in Latin America until very recently. Regrettably, this process has not been corrected by existing governments which, in order to attract foreign investments, have generally waived environmental performance requirements.

NATIONAL TREATMENT PRINCIPLE

The national treatment principle, according to which host countries may not impose performance conditions on TNCs that are more stringent than those imposed on nationals, can have negative effects on the environment.

In so far as the long-term effects of environmental pollution are global, there is little justification for TNCs to invoke the national treatment principle to relieve themselves from what otherwise would constitute their normal responsibilities. The environmental standards imposed by home countries on transnational corporations are generally stricter than those applied by any Latin American country.[13] This laxness in the national treatment may be attributed to the perception of local governments that foreign investments will turn away from countries with strict environmental regulations.[14] Indeed, the opposite may be true as is demonstrated by the fact that the country with the most stringent environmental controls, the United States, is also the largest recipient of foreign investments. In addition, Leonard and Duerksen (1980, pp. 56-8) concluded that there was no evidence to indicate that low environmental standards were a consideration in the decisions of American TNCs for investing in developing countries. In certain industries, however, there is evidence that new investments have been directed to countries with lower environmental standards. This has been the case with industries producing highly toxic products (asbestos, benzidine, dyes and pesticides) and processing heavy metals (copper, zinc and lead) (United Nations Centre on Transnational Corporations, 1988, p. 230).

However, even in this situation, the decision to attract investments by lowering environmental controls or standards would not be beneficial to such countries in the long term and could have the opposite effect of inhibiting foreign investments in general.

A discouraging development in this area are the recent Bilateral Investment Treaties which, together with including the national treatment principle, prohibit the imposition by host governments of performance requirements as a condition for the establishment, expansion or maintenance of investments. Moreover, these treaties make no reference to environmental protection. An unfortunate consequence of these treaties will probably be the weakening of the efforts of host governments for enhancing environmental standards.

ENTERPRISE FOR THE AMERICAS

The operation of President Bush's Enterprise for the Americas Initiative is expected to expand Latin American trade and increase foreign investments which will confer on TNCs a critical responsibility towards the environment. This issue has drawn particular attention during the recent negotiations of the North American Free Trade Agreement of August 1992 between the United States, Canada and Mexico.

To ensure that TNCs comply with appropriate environmental standards in Latin America, the following measures should be considered:

- the adoption of an environmental code of conduct for TNCs;
- the acceptance of responsibility by parent companies for the activities of their subsidiaries or affiliates;
- compliance by TNCs in Latin America with the environmental standards of their home countries; and
- *ex ante* review by host governments of the environmental impact of foreign investment projects or operations.

PPP can be one of the policy instruments which countries may apply to reduce the negative environmental impact of TNC activities. However, it may not be a solution, but only a supplement to other regulatory measures.

CONCLUSIONS

On account of the differences in the nature of the environmental problems of both regions, the impact of the application of PPP in Latin America would not be as significant as in OECD countries. Its impact on the export prices of manufactures and primary commodities raises complex trade issues, whose consequences need to be carefully assessed prior to its adoption.

If adopted, PPP should be an integral component of a comprehensive case-by-case sustainable development policy which includes the enactment of appropriate legislation and the establishment or reinforcement of the corresponding institutions. Technical cooperation for capacity building should be instrumental to its successful execution. Transition to an open-market economy raises difficulties and highlights the importance of defining the PPP area of application *vis-à-vis* other environmental policy instruments. The significance of environmental degradation in the Latin American region, as distinguished from industrial pollution, and the application of PPP are critical issues which require careful analysis.

Privatization, technology transfer, foreign investment, expansion of trade, intellectual property rights in the countries of Latin America and the Caribbean and the operations of TNCs also raise significant environmental issues that would have to be taken into consideration in the application of PPP.

ANNEX A

Recent Legislation of Latin American Countries

As a result of its adoption by the United Nations Conference on Water Resources of 1977 in Mar del Plata, Argentina, an embryonic PPP has been included in the water pollution legislation of some Latin American countries. There is, however, very little information on the degree of compliance and/or of enforcement of this legislation. Among the examples that may be cited are:

Argentina

Federal Decree No. 674 of 24 May 1989, which regulates the industrial pollution of water resources in the Province of Buenos Aires. The decree classifies industrial effluents in three categories: (i) those which remain within permissible limits and are not subject to the payment of special charges; (ii) those temporarily tolerated (no longer than two years) but which do not exceed an established limit of concentration and on which special charges are imposed; and (iii) those prohibited because they exceed the tolerable limits of contamination and are subject to punitive measures which may lead to the closure of the industry. The charges collected are used to finance the control system which is administered by the federal water agency (Empresa Obras Sanitarias de la Nación) and community participation is recognized by the establishment of a public registry for denunciations (see Flory, 1989, pp. 11-16).

Venezuela

Resolution 124 of 21 December 1984,[15] approved the regulations for the control of pollution of Lake Valencia. This resolution classifies the industrial activities and pollution limits of the effluents that may be discharged into the lake. Non-compliance, however, is not automatically sanctioned as time-limits of up to 180 days which can be extended are given for compliance. The resolution does not establish the payment of special charges as in the case of Argentina, mentioned above.

Mexico

A special law enacted in 1991 regulates the discharge of effluents and solids into the water resources of the nation including rivers, oceans and subterranean waters. Special charges in fixed amounts in local currency are established which fluctuate in accordance with the volume or weight of the pollutant. There is no reference, however, to a prohibitive limit of contamination or a qualitative classification of the pollutants. The revenues collected through the law will be allocated to cover the budget expenses contemplated for this purpose for the Water Commission, and any surplus will be returned to the Treasury.

Uruguay

Special legislation has been enacted since 1978 to control the contamination of water resources. Pursuant to this legislation,[16] the Service of Environmental Management of the Ministry of Transportation and Public Works supervises the enforcement of this legislation. The system regulates the discharge of effluents into all the water resources of the country, requires industries to submit for government approval the construction of treatment plants and establishes penalties for non-compliance. Technically, however, these regulations do not include the establishment of PPP as no charges, based on the type of pollutant, are applied.

ANNEX B

Water Resources[17]

The region possesses what are among the largest riverways and river basins in the world which include the Orinoco, Amazon, Parana and Magdalena rivers. However, although Latin America and the Caribbean have abundant water resources, their populations suffer from scarcity because these resources are generally located far away from the great urban centres or industries.

The region has an annual average rainfall of 1,500 mm which is 50 per cent higher than the world average. It also contributes almost onethird (370,000 m³/sec) of the world-wide land drainage entering the oceans. Pollution of the water resources of the region has, for this reason, an immediate impact on the marine environment and world's oceans in general.

In spite of the great water potential, its utilization is very low. Thus, in the early 1980s, only about 3 per cent of the surface water was used for consumption, while the installed hydroelectric capacity represented less than 7 per cent of the estimated hydroelectric potential. Only about 8 per cent of the arable land was irrigated, even though about one fourth was estimated to require some form of irrigation. However, the region's proven hydropower reserves amount to 2,700 million Gwh, almost equal to its petroleum reserves and exceeding those of natural gas. It thus represents a major asset as a source of renewable energy.

The major problems of water pollution in the region arise from the drainage of industrial and mining wastes in waterways, lack of treatment of sewage effluents in the great urban centres and intensive use of fertilizers, herbicides and pesticides. In more recent years, mining for gold in the Peruvian and Brazilian Amazon, which generates silt, oil and mercury, has also contributed to river contamination. A similar but even more serious problem is the pollution of rivers caused by the manufacture of coca paste in the Andean highlands which is then exported to produce cocaine. According to a 1987 calculation, coca growers dump the following volumes of toxic chemicals annually in the Peruvian Amazon: 15 million gallons of kerosene, 8 million gallons of sulphuric acid, 1.6 million gallons of acetone, 1.6 million gallons of the solvent toluene, 16,000 tons of lime and 3,200 tons of carbide (Dourojeanni, 1989).

NOTES

1 This paper represents the opinions of the author and not necessarily those of the Inter-American Development Bank (IDB).
2 Plato, 1953 The reference to Plato was made by the Undersecretary of Foreign Affairs of Chile, Edmundo Vargas, at a seminar organized by the Organization of American States on Trade and the Environment, April 1992, Santiago, Chile.
3 PPP was adopted by the OECD in 1972 and means, according to its Council, 'that the polluter should bear the expenses of carrying out the measures (for allocating costs of pollution prevention and control), to ensure that the environment is in an acceptable state', and that 'the cost of these measures should be reflected in the cost of goods and services which cause pollution in production and/or consumption'. In the Council's estimation its application should not include subsidies but 'encourage the rational use and the better allocation of scarce environmental resources and prevent the appearance of distortions in international trade and investment' (Annex 1, 'Recommendation'). UPP is a broader principle concerned with the depletion of exhaustible resources rather than pollution and which states that the user should pay for the full cost of the resource and its related services.
4 In the case of the United States, it has been estimated that compliance with recently enacted environmental laws would raise pollution control expenses to the equivalent of 3 or 4 per cent of its GDP (see UNCED, 1992a, p. 6, para. 22).
5 The commodity terms of trade, measured as the ratio of the index of commodity prices to that of

manufactured goods, dropped nearly 40 per cent between 1980 and 1986, and the region's terms of trade in 1989 were 21 per cent below their level of 1980 (see IDB, 1991, p. 5).

6   The OECD Convention was signed in Paris on 14 December 1960; its members include the 24 most industrialized countries. Its Council has the power to adopt binding decisions and non-binding recommendations on environmental and other matters.

7   This can, of course, change in the future and, indeed, the MERCOSUR ('Mercado Común del Sur') treaty of Asunción, Paraguay, of 26 March 1991, between Argentina, Brazil, Uruguay and Paraguay, could become an appropriate instrument for the implementation of environmental policies in those countries.

8   In Brazil, for example, research on this subject found no evidence that criminal penalties or indictments had been imposed for water pollution (see Leme Machado, 1989, p. 259).

9   On the absence of environmental policies in Brazil, Colombia, Ecuador and Chile, see the following: in Brazil, Filgueiras Cavalcante, 1991; in Colombia, Arrubla Pancar 1991 ibid; in Ecuador, Fundación Natura,1991; in Chile, Asenjo and Torres, 1991, pp. 70-83.

10   The principle of objective responsibility for damages to the environment has been recognized in Article 225(3) of the Federal Constitution of Brazil of 1988 and Article 14 (1) of the National Law for Environmental Policy ('Lei de Politica Nacional do Meio Ambiente').

11   In 1990, the share of exports was as follows: non-fuel primary commodities, 41.2%; mineral fuels, 24.4%; manufactures, 33.5%. (United Nations Statistical Office, 1990, Table 1.1: Structure of Latin American Trade by Major Product Category).

12   To redress the pollution problems of chemical discharges into the San Juan and Mantaro rivers, the IDB gave a special loan to CENTROMIN-Peru in December 1976 for the construction of a water treatment and neutralization plant.

13   A report issued in 1979 on the basis of interviews of 317 American enterprises cited Latin America as having the most lax controls (see Koo *et al.*, 1979, Chap. V).

14   Some foreign investment statutes have no provisions related to the environment. In the case of Chile, Ortuzar (1992, p. 3) has stated: 'The Foreign Investments Committee ... is not empowered ... to impose environmental protection rules that may apply to the investors ... '.

15   Amended by resolution of 8 January 1985, published in the Official Gazette of 30 January 1985.

16   Decree-law No. 14859 of 28 December 1978, decree 253 of 9 May 1979, law No. 15903 of 18 December 1987, and decree of 17 March 1988.

17   Data in this section draw from the IDB, 1983, pp. 37-54.

7. NATURAL RESOURCE MANAGEMENT AND THE PRECAUTIONARY PRINCIPLE

Anthony H. Chisholm and Harry R. Clarke

INTRODUCTION

The Precautionary Principle (PP) suggests that: 'Where there are threats of serious or irreversible damage, lack of full scientific certainty should not be used as a reason for postponing measures to prevent environmental degradation.' (Bergen Ministerial Declaration, 1990).

It has been proposed that PP should be adopted as a guiding policy for international environmental negotiations. Environmental policies based on PP and designed to achieve sustainable development would: 'anticipate, prevent and attack the causes of environmental degradation' (Bergen Ministerial Declaration, 1990).

In relation to the issue of climate change, PP is understood as suggesting that there is a case for restricting carbon dioxide and other greenhouse gas emissions *now* even if there is no scientific certainty that these emissions are contributing to greenhouse problems *and* no certainty regarding the extent of costs even if greenhouse effects should arise. As Cameron and Werksman (1991, p. 2) argue: 'a precautionary regime demands that the greenhouse hypothesis be accepted and that action be taken now'. These same authors argue that PP will have special appeal to developing countries because they will suffer the greatest losses should climatic change occur.

In this chapter, the prospect of an enhanced greenhouse effect (EGE) is used as a vehicle to try to provide a rationale for PP. The greenhouse effect is a natural phenomenon, but emissions resulting from human activities are increasing the concentrations of the greenhouse gases: carbon dioxide, methane, chlorofluorocarbons and nitrous oxides.[1] These emissions will enhance the greenhouse effect. The EGE has the characteristic of a truly global public good. The impact of an EGE on any nation or region depends solely on the global concentrations of greenhouse gas emissions and it is quite independent of the share of the total is attributable to a nation's own emissions. The issue here is first approached as being one of decision-making under risk and is then appraised, perhaps more realistically, in a framework of uncertainty. Initially, it is assumed that there is some symmetry between the costs and benefits facing developing and developed countries in a global environmental agreement. The discussion then proceeds to consider the implications for developing countries when the developed countries effectively bear the full costs of any global agreement to reduce greenhouse gas emissions.

Agriculture, together with forestry and fisheries, are the major sectors likely to be affected by climatic change. Agriculture plays an especially large role in the economic life of developing countries. Thus, despite increasing levels of international economic integration, susceptibility of developing countries to climate change is likely to be much greater than for most developed countries. Bangladesh and a number of island economies are directly threatened by the potentially devastating effects of a rise in sea-level. Most importantly, developing countries have a lower capacity than developed countries to adapt in the face of climatic change. For this reason policy-makers in developing countries are likely to be more risk averse than those in developed countries.

The fact that agriculture in developed countries is only a small share of GNP should not be construed as meaning that any threat to food consumption is relatively unimportant for developed countries. In developed countries there is a very large consumer surplus associated with their current levels of food consumption at existing prices. Consequently, the willingness of developed countries to pay to maintain their current levels of food consumption means that any reduction of global food production caused by an EGE and resulting in higher world prices would have the major impact of lowering food consumption in the poorer developing countries.

In many instances, actions to combat local environmental problems, protect biodiversity, and so forth, will simultaneously have a desirable impact on EGE. Conversely, policies aimed at combating EGE, such as reducing forms of air pollution caused by using fossil fuels and the lowering of clear-felling of native forests, will also often help alleviate local environmental problems. It may also be argued that there is considerable potential for those Eastern European countries moving towards a market-based economy to introduce new and more efficient production technologies, which, by economizing on energy inputs, are also less polluting.

The above types of policy, which serve a dual purpose (sometimes termed 'all-weather' or 'minimum-regret' policies), are particularly attractive if there is a significant chance that either a greenhouse problem will not occur or that human preventive action will be ineffective.

It is also important to note that short-term political time horizons are likely to intrude as principal determinants of what is feasible in terms of dealing with potential EGE hazards. According to Schelling (1992), EGE effects are likely to accrue gradually over time. The decision task facing democratic governments then is whether or not to incur very large costs now to offset potentially even larger costs accumulating over some lengthy and distant future period. Politically, the 'salient' or 'vivid' costs (to use Akerlof's (1991) characterization) are current rather than future costs. This myopia provides incentives for decision-makers to delay or to 'procrastinate' and it is this very procrastination itself which provides a basis for negotiating PP as an inflexible global rule via, e.g., an international agreement which forces governments to act immediately. This increases global social welfare since procrastination does not lead to a maximization of 'true' welfare.

RATIONALE FOR THE PRECAUTIONARY PRINCIPLE

As a first attempt to solve the EGE problem, the appropriate economic objective might be presented as one of minimizing the present value of expected total damage plus abatement costs. The optimal policy principle would then require that at each moment of time, emissions of greenhouse gases should be reduced to the point where the current marginal cost of abatement equals the present value of marginal expected damage costs. The expected present value approach then gives weight to all possible values of marginal damages according to the current likelihood of their occurrence.

This approach, however, assumes government to be risk neutral, typically on the premiss that a single project is small relative to the whole economy, and that government can accordingly use its tax powers to ensure that no matter how risky the project is, no individual is exposed to significant risk. However, this is an unrealistic assumption for environmental problems such as EGE, since the downside risks could involve catastrophic damages causing dramatic reductions in an individual's well being no matter how widely risks were shared across an economy or globally.

We therefore begin our survey of possible theoretical rationales for PP by surveying decision procedures which explicitly account for risk-aversion. Subsequently we show that risk-neutrality can be a useful assumption for deducing clearly the effects of risk and irreversibility by means of the quasi-option value concept.[2]

Expected Utility

Expected utility theory (EUT) provides the conventional economic framework for rational choice under risk when the assumption of risk-neutrality is relaxed. The theory is useful for dealing with situations in which probabilities and possible outcomes are within the normal range of human experience. With risk-aversion, individuals place more weight on the disutility of damages caused by an EGE than they would if they were risk neutral and maximized expected value. Consequently, EUT will select a policy that is more strongly orientated toward a precautionary approach with a lower level of greenhouse gas emissions than in the risk-neutral case.

However, a major feature of most differences between the observed choices made by people in carefully constructed experiments and 'rational' choices based on EUT is that people place greater weight on low-probability extreme events than the theory predicts (Quiggin, 1982). That is to say, some axioms are consistently violated in experimental research. This suggests that EUT may not provide an adequate framework for explaining and predicting social choice in risky situations where there are very low probabilities of extreme (perhaps catastrophic) events.

Moreover, it is argued by Loomes and Sugden (1982), for example, that EUT represents an unnecessarily restrictive notion of rationality and that it is no less rational to act in accordance with the notion of 'regret'. This implies that in some situations EUT may give too little weight to risk-aversion. In contrast, the corresponding minimax model under uncertainty, which is discussed in the following section, essentially allows risk-aversion to become infinite.

Uncertainty and the Minimax Strategy

Risk refers to the circumstances where at least subjective probabilities can be assigned to states of the world. Uncertainty is usually interpreted to mean that states of the world are known but that probabilities cannot be assigned. Uncertainty would appear to be a more realistic framework than risk for analysing the EGE problem. Apart from the anticipated higher temperature and associated sea-level rise, there are fundamental uncertainties regarding the impact of EGE on the stability of the climate-biosphere system.

Since PP emphasizes the irreversibility associated with climate change costs in a context of uncertainty, it is natural to look at the framework of decision theory for a rationale. Like classical decision theory, adopting PP implies acting to avoid unfavourable events regardless of their likelihood.

Ready and Bishop (1991) attempt to unravel the relationship between rules of the PP type and classical decision analysis in another environmental context.

We follow their lead and interpret the EGE policy problem as a two-person game against nature.

Suppose a country has to choose between PP and no action, which we designate continued development (DEV). The costs of adopting PP, denoted C, include both the direct costs of the policy and the social cost of output forgone. We initially consider two possible future 'states of the world':

S_1 = event that EGE damages (L) are very large in the absence of PP
S_2 = event that EGE damages are insignificant in the absence of PP.

If we take as the benchmark case the situation where PP is adopted and large damages are averted, we can derive the following loss matrix:

	State		
Strategy	S_1	S_2	Max Loss
PP	0	0	0
DEV	$L - C$	$-C$	$L - C$

Assuming that $C < L$, a policy rule which attempts to avoid the maximum possible loss (the minimax strategy) involves always selecting PP and thus avoiding the worst possible outcome, $L - C$. This policy outcome is relevant in the situation Ready and Bishop refer to as the 'insurance game', where the only uncertainty relates to the magnitude of the damages caused by EGE.

It may however be argued that another type of uncertainty is whether or not PP will be effective. Ready and Bishop refer to such situations as a 'lottery game'. Suppose now that in the absence of PP we know with certainty that large EGE damages will be incurred, but if we implement PP it may or may not be effective. In the loss matrix shown below, S_3 denotes a state where PP is ineffective.

	State			
Strategy	S_1	S_2	S_3	Max Loss
PP	0	0	L	L
DEV	$L - C$	$-C$	$L - C$	$L - C$

If we initially suppress the state of the world S_2 and consider the pure 'lottery game' it can be seen that PP is not the appropriate policy when the minimax principle is applied. The reason is that the worst possible outcome that can now occur is that implementation of a costly PP fails to avert large EGE damages.

Considering all three possible states of the world, the case for PP as a means of avoiding the worst possible outcome is again overturned. If there is uncertainty about whether or not PP will be effective, the worst that can happen is that we should incur costs in an attempt to control greenhouse emissions only to find that climate change occurs regardless. The general point we are making here parallels that made by Ready and Bishop. Unless there is no uncertainty associated with the effectiveness of PP, we cannot rationalize PP as being the appropriate minimax strategy in a two-person game against nature.

Minimax Regret Strategy

As Ready and Bishop argue, it is possible to justify a policy like PP if a minimax regret decision rule is applied. This is a strategy in which society seeks to minimize its regrets for not having, in hindsight, made the superior choice. The strategy could be interpreted as implying the taking of a decision now which current generations believe future generations would least regret. Cameron and Werksman (1991, p. 22) cite the US Secretary of State as, in fact, advocating a 'no-regrets' policy which seems to come close to this.

The minimum regret cost matrix for the game presented is:

		State		
Strategy	S_1	S_2	S_3	Max Regret
PP	0	C	C	C
DEV	$L-C$	0	0	$L-C$

Thus the maximum regret incurred with PP arises either when it is ineffective, or, when with the benefit of hindsight, it was unnecessary. The maximum regret incurred with DEV is the loss incurred when EGE causes large damages which could have been avoided by PP. Comparing these regrets, if:

$$L - C > C$$
i.e. $$L > 2C$$

then PP should be implemented on the basis of a minimax regret policy.

On the one hand, compared with the minimax decision rule, the minimax regret rule is commonly criticized on the grounds that regret consists of 'crying over spilt milk', which the proverb says is not the way to optimize. However, by posing the decision-task as a 'lottery game' it seems that strict application of the minimax decision rule can lead to a quite different choice. No matter how small the cost of PP, if there is the slightest uncertainty that PP will not be effective it will not be selected by the minimax decision rule.

The minimax regret rule, on the other hand, sensibly gives some weight to the relationship between the costs of PP and the losses incurred, with no action being taken when EGE damages are large. In particular, if the costs of EGE damages exceed twice the costs of PP, it should be implemented even though there is uncertainty about whether or not it will be effective. The minimax regret rule would thus tend to favour 'all-weather' policies which serve a dual purpose, such as reducing inefficient energy use as well as greenhouse gas emissions.

Quasi-option Value and PP

Another important argument supporting a precautionary approach arises, even if decision-makers are risk neutral, provided that irreversibilities exist and it is possible to learn through time about the costs and benefits of controlling greenhouse gas emissions. Carbon dioxide has a residence time in the atmosphere of a century or more. Moreover, even if after a long time-lag, concentrations of greenhouse gases in the atmosphere were reduced from a level which had caused substantial damages, for example in the form of sea-level rise and flooding of low-lying land, such damages are likely to be largely irreversible. Where the irreversibility is associated with not taking action now (a 'sin of omission'), and there is considerable uncertainty about the damages caused by different levels of greenhouse gas concentrations, there is a case for being even more conservative in relation to emission controls than would be suggested by applying the minimax principle.

This latter result can be rationalized in terms of the concept of quasi-option value originally put forward by Arrow and Fisher (1974) and subsequently developed by Fisher and Hanemann (1986, 1990). Thus, whenever a decision has the characteristic that one of the possible outcomes is irreversible, and there is a prospect of learning and gaining better information with the passage of time then, even in the absence of risk-aversion, the balance is tilted in favour of action that maintains flexibility by retaining the option to 'preserve' or develop in the future. If we control greenhouse gas emissions now and subsequently learn that we were not at a threshold of irreversible damage, we can always resume development; but if we do not control those emissions now and subsequently discover that we were at a threshold of upward irreversibility, the damage cannot be undone by subsequent increased controls.

As suggested by Fisher and Hanemann (1986) in another environmental context, an implication of upward irreversibility for greenhouse gas emission controls is that it leads to a case for anticipatory rather than purely reactive policies. Thus, excluding the possibility that PP is ineffective (i.e. excluding

S_3), the minimax principle would suggest the optimality of control when $L >$ C. However, the existence of a quasi-option value (QOV) associated with avoiding an upwardly irreversible threshold will inevitably imply the optimality of acting to thwart an EGE threat in circumstances where $L < C$ even in the absence of risk-aversion. On the one hand, incurring EGE damages involves an irreversible loss of options since once such damages occur it will be difficult or impossible to remedy the situation. On the other hand, adopting PP and forgoing development is a policy which can be reversed in the future. Thus adoption of DEV involves an asymmetric loss of options which has economic value (equal to QOV) so that action to prevent EGE will be optimal when C exceeds L by less than QOV.

Of course a precautionary approach aimed at acquiring better information depends on more than the mere passage of time. Investment in research on the likely benefits of controls is required to obtain a finer resolution of uncertainty.

Developing Countries and PP

Most observers believe that whatever is done to reduce the EGE will need to be almost wholly financed by the high-income developed countries. Developing countries, and many previously socialist Eastern European countries, have pressing local and regional pollution problems. Pollution of air, water and soil in these regions is at the present time seriously degrading the environment and causing human illness and death. It is unrealistic to expect these countries to support any international agreement that will have a payoff (reduced EGE) in 50 to 75 years if such action reduces the resources available to combat regional pollution and environmental problems that are having serious impacts here and now. The discount rates that apply in developing countries are higher than those in developed countries. Thus, developing countries are likely to invest their resources and undertake research only in 'all-weather' policies to abate the EGE.

Despite the apparent 'need' for developed countries to finance global efforts to offset EGE, some see the asymmetric distribution of benefits from such actions as potentially inhibiting action. Thus Schelling (1992) puts forward a carefully argued view that the economic impact of EGE on developed countries is likely to be negligible – at least if, as he supposes, EGE changes are gradual rather than catastrophic in nature. However, this complacent assessment cannot be extended to the developing world because of what we earlier described as its agricultural bias. Thus, from the viewpoint of self-interest, why should the developed countries do anything? One must look towards altruism or some alternative basis of self-interest (protection of genetic resources or insurance against catastrophic EGE-induced changes) to be assured that developed countries will meet funding needs.

If for the sake of argument we now assume that the cost of a global PP is fully borne by the high-income developed countries, we obtain the following loss matrix for developing countries:

	State		
	S_1	S_2	S_3
PP	0	0	L
DEV	L	0	L

Not surprisingly, a precautionary greenhouse policy would be favoured by developing countries if the cost of global PP is entirely met by developed countries. Even though maximum losses are the same with both policies, these losses are realized only when a single state of the world eventuates with PP (namely S_3). However, they are realized when either S_1 or S_3 eventuates under DEV. It is pertinent to note that if the developing countries had to bear even a tiny share of the cost of a global PP, the above loss matrix would show that the minimax decision rule would select DEV. This conclusion is related to the earlier argument that if there is the slightest uncertainty that PP will be ineffective it will not be selected by the minimax decision rule (no matter how small the cost of the PP) and this rigidity reflects a weakness of the rule. It seems likely that developing countries would be expected to bear some fraction of the cost of a global PP (at least in terms of forgone output) to combat the EGE.

However, as long as per capita incomes and greenhouse emission levels in developing countries remain substantially below those in developed countries, it appears inequitable (if not entirely unlikely) that any global greenhouse agreement would require substantial sacrifices in economic growth by developing countries. Indeed, if there is some chance that a global policy to combat greenhouse emissions will be ineffective, it may be argued that strong economic growth, which would reduce the dependence of developing economies on their agricultural sectors, is a highly effective adaptive action these countries can take towards possible future climatic change. Similarly, application of the Precautionary Principle to developing countries must give prominence to combating local and regional pollution and environmental problems with potentially serious and irreversible consequences. It follows that a significant contribution of developing countries to a global PP for combating the EGE should be in terms of all-weather policies, which serve the dual purpose of increasing efficiencies of energy and resource use by reducing emissions of greenhouse gases.

POLICY INSTRUMENTS

It is beyond the scope of this chapter to provide a detailed discussion of the various policy instruments that may be used to protect the environment.[3] These issues are addressed in related papers in this series on the Polluter-Pays and User-Pays Principles.

From an economics perspective, several essential characteristics of an efficient solution to a pollution/environmental problem may be identified. Firstly, for each type of pollution, the marginal costs of pollution abatement should be equal for all pollution sources. Secondly, where adaptation is possible, the social return from investment in mitigation strategies should, at the margin, be balanced with the return from investment in adaptive strategies. Thirdly, policies should provide a continuous incentive through time towards technological change and adaptation towards more efficient (less costly) ways of controlling pollution. Fourthly, the administrative costs, comprising mainly information costs and monitoring and enforcement costs, should not be excessive. Environmental policies based on the above criteria will achieve outcomes such that the sum of pollution damages plus pollution abatement costs is kept to a minimum.

Traditional instruments for control of environmental risks commonly rely on legal liability, in various forms, after risky events have actually occurred. There is increasing concern that private decision-makers do not perceive themselves as having to bear the full social costs of risky behaviour under this form of regulation. Farber (1991) provides several reasons why this may be true. Perhaps the most compelling is that firms know they have the option of bankruptcy when damage liabilities exceed assets thereby limiting overall liabilities. Moreover, remote risks may be discoverable only after costly research, and firms may have an incentive to limit their knowledge of this type of risk particularly in order to claim ignorance as a defence against liability.

Menell (1991), a Professor of Law, also argues that the attributes of legal institutions, particularly in the area of legal regulation and liability, significantly limit their effectiveness in prospectively regulating pollution emissions and retrospectively attaining clean-up of pollution, such as that arising from abandoned hazardous waste sites. Menell claims, for instance, that the two principal systems of environmental liability in the United States – the toxic tort system and the Superfund Law – are poorly suited to addressing problems of environmental risks in which there is a high level of scientific uncertainty about causation and where there are many potentially responsible parties. The perceived weaknesses of existing systems of legal environmental liability, together with the typically high cost of court hearings on liability for environmental damages, have led many observers, including Menell, to argue for increased use of administered and market-based incentives as a means of protecting the environment. 'The objectives of efficient deterrence of environmental harms can be furthered by reducing the role of legal institutions and appropriately increasing the roles of administrative and market institutions' (Menell, 1991, p. 111).

Two schemes that have been proposed to combat the EGE problem and which appear to have many of the desirable efficiency characteristics are transferable emission permits and carbon taxes. These schemes can be structured to attain both efficiency and distributional goals. Whalley and Wigle (1990), for instance, use an applied general equilibrium model of the world economy to examine the implications of alternative carbon taxation regimes to secure a 50 per cent reduction in global carbon dioxide emissions arising from fossil fuel combustion. They obtain the result that the least global (total) cost option involves redistributing the tax revenue raised to nations on an equal per capita basis. The developing/centrally–planned group of countries is a net gainer (1.8 per cent increase in GDP) after such an allocation. The developing countries gain because the developed countries generate a higher level of carbon dioxide emissions per capita and there is thus a transfer of tax revenues from the developed to the developing countries. A system which redistributes carbon tax revenues between countries on an equal per capita basis would appear to provide incentives for excessive population growth in developing countries. Discussions of other global targets and schemes are contained in Barrett (1990), Cline (1991), and Pearce (1991).

Work by UNCTAD (1992) on a global system of tradable carbon emission entitlements (tradable permits) examines efficiency gains and distributional goals as integrated objectives. This study goes beyond the conventional allocation rules such as 'grandfathering', population, land area, and efficiency (GNP) criteria, and examines the distributional impact of: weighted averages (e.g. between per capita CO_2 emissions and uniform percentage reductions); two-tier and multi-tier allocations; and the application of moral principles (kantian rule). (See also recent works by the World Bank (1992) and OECD (1992 a and b).

CONCLUDING COMMENTS

In this chapter the relation between alternative decision procedures (expected value maximization, expected utility maximization and classical decision theory) and the heuristically plausible PP has been examined. PP has been proposed as a guide to taking environmental decisions so it is of interest to see how it is linked to more formal decision-making techniques.

What has been observed is that, even with risk-neutrality, there is a substantial case for taking anticipatory policy actions whenever there is the prospect that the failure to take policy actions involves substantial irreversible costs.

In an uncertainty context the link between conservative decision-making rules such as minimax and the PP is seen to depend on the source of uncertainty in an environmental system. If uncertainty is concentrated entirely on the issue of whether greenhouse problems will or will not occur ('insurance game'), then PP policies will be selected whenever greenhouse costs are anticipated to exceed costs of policy action. If, however, uncertainty also bears on the issue of whether or not PP policies themselves will be effective ('lottery game'), then (following Ready and Bishop, 1991) the minimax policy principle always implies abandoning PP, regardless of how small the cost of PP is. In the latter case, the minimax regret strategy will select PP if the social losses for the worst possible scenario are at least twice as large as the costs of PP.

Each of the above approaches to decision-making under uncertainty, by making specific informational assumptions, has weaknesses which highlight the crucial importance of information in taking sensible decisions. For instance, in the 'insurance game' the minimax strategy can be an unduly conservative rule. On the one hand, if the costs of implementing PP are only slightly less than the social losses that would be incurred under the worst possible scenario, then PP will be selected regardless of how small the chance is of that state occurring. On the other hand, in the 'lottery game' the minimax strategy always selects the development alternative regardless of how small the cost of PP and how small the chance that it will not be effective. Clearly, in these circumstances, any probability information about the likelihood of alternative scenarios (states) eventuating and the associated costs and benefits of alternative policies would be most valuable.

Probability information will almost certainly be primarily subjective since 'frequentist' measures based on past experience and experiment are very difficult to derive. If pilot studies and simulations based on complex models are feasible then they should be used to narrow the range of probability distributions that need to be considered. Moreover, in attempting to aggregate the alternative community perceptions on subjective probability estimation using such studies, there is a well-known case for using the most-informed public information based on expert advice rather than information which reflects private views. While individual preferences over allocations at each state of the world might be respected this might not be the case regarding their subjective probability views. Protection from the EGE is a 'merit good' (i.e. a good the provision of which society wishes to encourage) and there is a case for justifying policies on the basis of well-informed opinion using the *Allais* type of equilibrium concept.[4]

What is inevitably difficult is the issue of aggregating alternative divergent subjective probability views. As Dasgupta (1982, p. 68) remarks:

> The language of probabilities is the natural one to use in dealing with uncertainty, even although in the case of environmental problems the probabilities will often be *subjective* ones. However, being subjective estimates, even experts disagree – often sharply – about the probable environmental effects of economic activities. Indeed if there is a hallmark of environmental debates it is precisely this.

This is very relevant in EGE debates. Thus as Ayres (1991) remarks in his critique of a well-known study by Nordhaus (1990):

> Nordhaus' paper implicitly assumes that a higher temperature and associated sea-level rise are the only consequences worth considering. Nordhaus altogether ignores the more fundamental uncertainties regarding the stability of the climate-biosphere system (the hydrological cycle, the nitrogen cycle, species diversity, etc.)[5];

and

> one must recognize at least the chance of a planetary extinction as great as the event or events which killed off the dinosaurs 70 million years ago. This is not to suggest it will happen; only that no one can be sure that it will *not* happen. Nor can the quantitative probabilities be determined.

It does seem desirable to at least reach agreement on excluding from consideration exceedingly unlikely events. All analysis takes place within some frame of reference since it is impossible to account for every possible eventuality. Cameron and Werksman (1991, p. 20) note that any definition of PP must include an 'evidentiary threshold' which implies that there is a significant probability that a particular action (e.g. continued development) will cause serious social damages or costs. This means that so long as social damages are not infinite for the worst conceivable event, that society should tolerate an evidentiary threshold below which environmental controls are not imposed even where it is the case that imposing such controls reduces literally to zero the probability of that event occurring. It is impossible to accept seriously the literal prescription that PP implies a case for environmental action whenever there is *any* prospect of significant damages.

We also have some guiding principles governing the provision of information which we believe may be useful in reducing the less extreme uncertainties. Such information is a public good which will be typically underprovided by markets. There is a case for its public provision. Some of this information can be drawn on as a 'common pool' so that, for developing countries in particular, research efforts should form a balance between maintaining an ability to skilfully draw on this pool and in developing specific local research programmes which address regional needs. As is well known, the value of information can be decreasing in the neighbourhood of low information levels, implying that research strategies should target the economies of scale that arise from specialized research programmmes which target specifically local needs.

Finally, because of past emissions of greenhouse gases and the long lags involved, it should be kept in mind that whatever abatement policies are now put in place some global warming is expected to occur. Research and policies therefore need to strike an appropriate balance between abatement and adaptive measures.

NOTES

1 For a good account of the scientific basis for the greenhouse effect see Cline (1991). It is interesting to note that Cline claims that over a long-time horizon of 250 to 300 years the stakes of global warming are closer to a central estimate of 10°C rather than the 2.5°C associated with the benchmark doubling of CO^2 which has so far dominated both scientific and policy discussion.

2 For a general review of issues of risk, uncertainty, irreversibility and sustainable resource use, see Chisholm (1988) and Clarke (1991).

3 For discussion and analysis of policy instruments to combat the EGE, see Barrett (1990), Mohr (1991), Pearce (1991), and Whalley and Wigle (1990).

4 See Dasgupta (1982, pp. 68-70) for a discussion of the role of expert opinion in utilizing the '*Allais* equilibrium' concept. An *Allais* or *ex post* equilibrium involves the government aggregating individual preferences over allocations in various states of nature using probability weights based on informed public information.

5 Nordhaus appears to overlook the likelihood of thresholds, relating to the rate of global warming, beyond which some species and ecosystems may cease to exist. Quiggin and Horowitz (1992) argue that Nordhaus (1990) does not make an explicit distinction between comparative static and dynamic estimates in his analyses of the likely costs and benefits of the EGE. In particular, examination of Nordhaus' damage estimates for agriculture reveal that they are based on a comparative static framework, and Quiggin and Horowitz claim that this leads to a significant underestimate of damages. They argue that the EGE introduces a new source of uncertainty and that the problem of adjustment costs can only be fully addressed by incorporating the uncertainty into a dynamic model.

8. THE SUBSIDIARITY PRINCIPLE

Michael Bothe

THE SUBSIDIARITY PRINCIPLE: ORIGINS AND CONTENT

The Subsidiarity Principle is generally invoked where a case is made for decisions to be taken at the lowest possible level. In this sense, it is used as a principle of organization in both the social and political fields. Where possible, decisions should be taken by the individual and/or the family, not by society at large; by the local community, not by the state; and by the Member states of a federation, not by the federation (Frenkel, 1984, p. 86 *et seq.*). The principle can also be applied where a choice has to be made between national and international regulations.

The roots of and justification for the Subsidiarity Principle can be found in three different sources. Firstly, it is said that the principle was developed by catholic social philosophy (Marcic, 1957, p. 428 *et seq*) but this is too narrow an explanation (Frenkel, 1984, p. 86 *et seq.*). The old philosophical idea of personal autonomy is behind the principle and is transferred into social and political organization. A second source is political and constitutional theory: the principle of democracy requires decisions to be taken close to the citizen and with citizen participation. It is in this sense and for this reason that the principle appears in the Council of Europe's European Charter of local self-government. Thirdly, on a practical level, it is argued that decision-making on a smaller scale is more efficient than decision-making in large units.

On these grounds, the Subsidiarity Principle is an element of argumentation in controversies about centralization versus decentralization in political systems. It is used to defend local autonomy against state power, or Member states of a federal state against the centre. It is used as a political weapon.

In controversies of this kind, where a central and a lower level of government compete for political power, the argument is often made that the Subsidiarity Principle is also part of positive law. It may be argued that it is inherent in the notion of federalism or in that of local autonomy. This is, to say the least, an inappropriate generalization. Subsidiarity means a preference for the lower level of decision-making. It means a burden of justification for centralization, or a kind of rebuttable presumption for decentralization (Frenkel, 1986, p. 111 *et seq.*). In the history of federal states, the political and constitutional battle for the appropriate problem-solving level has shifted in one way or the other. It would be a distortion of constitutional history and constitutional law to say that a preference for the lower level of government is generally inherent in the notion of a federal system. The trend in the federal systems of Europe and North America during the 1930s and after the Second World War leaned more towards centralization (Frenkel, 1986, p. 102 *et seq.*; Bothe, 1977, p. 272 *et seq.*). In recent years, there has been a renaissance of decentralization, of a greater role for Member states in federal systems, and of regionalism and localism (Bothe, 1987, p. 419 *et seq.*; Elazar, 1987, p. 201 *et seq.*; Ossenbühl, 1990, *passim*). There has been a rediscovery of subsidiarity (Constantinescu, 1991a, p. 439). The trend towards centralization was related to new concepts of state functions, in particular to the development of the welfare state. The rediscovery of subsidiarity is related to a more differentiated approach towards state regulation and towards the appropriate ways and means of solving the problems of modern society.

Various elements of the Subsidiarity Principle can be found in some constitutional systems. Under the German Basic Law, for instance, Article 72, a crucial provision concerning the division of legislative powers requires a 'need for federal legislation' where the federation wants to use its concurrent legislative powers. It is significant for the centralization trends of earlier years (Bothe, 1991a, p. 125 *et seq.*) that the German Constitutional Court declared the federal legislature to be the judge of this need, thus refusing a judicial review of it. It is also significant for the rediscovery of subsidiarity that in recent times some political forces want to revitalize Article 72 and, through constitutional amendment, force the court to pass judgement on the need for federal legislation.   Behind this controversy, there is also the question of the justiciability of the Subsidiarity Principle as part of positive law.

There are three principles of constitutional law in many federal states which are, to a certain extent, related to the idea of subsidiarity, although they have to be distinguished from it. The first is the principle of enumerated powers (Bothe, 1977, p. 137; Constantinescu, 1991a, p. 447). The federal level has only those powers which are specifically assigned to it by the constitution. The powers which are not enumerated (residual powers) are assigned to the Member states. The principle of enumerated powers is a formal one; it regulates the form in which the powers are divided between the two levels of government. It does not contain any substantative rules as to whether a preference should be given to either one or the other. It is, however, related to the Subsidiarity Principle in that it functions as a limit on federal powers.

The principle of implied powers is, secondly, connected with that of enumerated powers (Bothe, 1977, p. 143 *et seq.*). If implied powers are defined as those 'necessary and proper' for the execution of enumerated powers, there is again an element of subsidiarity, as the notion of 'necessary and proper' conveys the idea of limiting federal powers to what is essential.

The third principle is that of proportionality (Bleckmann and Bothe, 1986, p. 109). It is concerned more with the relationship between the state and the individual than with that between the state and lower levels of the government. But it has to be applied for example in constitutional systems where a guarantee of local autonomy is construed as a kind of fundamental right, which is, for instance, the case in Germany. The principle of proportionality limits the power of a legislature or other decision-maker to limit fundamental or other rights. It means that a limitation of a right is admissible only where it is necessary and appropriate to protect a competing societal value and where the disadvantage for the right which is limited is not disproportionate in relation to the advantage for the societal value to be protected. The principle of proportionality, in general, works as a restraint on state regulation. This brings it into the vicinity of the Subsidiarity Principle.

Regarding the protection of the environment, the principle of proportionality is relevant where the environment is a competing value in the sense just described, i.e. that it requires a limitation of other rights, mainly economic freedoms, particularly the freedom of international trade (or in some federal systems, interstate trade). Under the law of the EC, limiting the freedom of trade between the Member states is permissible only where it is necessary to protect other values – in this context, the environment – and if the advantage for the competing value (the 'environment') is proportionate to the negative impact on trade. This kind of question was, for example, involved in the well-known Danish Bottle case (Court of Justice of the European Communities, Report 1988, p. 4607 *et seq*). That case shows that the principle of proportionality is an important element in justifying national measures for the protection of the environment in a free-trade regime.

THE SUBSIDIARITY PRINCIPLE WITHIN THE FRAMEWORK OF THE EUROPEAN COMMUNITIES

The treaties establishing the European Communities provide for a system of enumerated powers. For a long time in the history of the Communities, the extent of the powers which remained with the Member state did not really present any problem. Community powers were (too) few anyway. Thus, there was no real need to discuss subsidiarity. That has changed and subsidiarity has become an issue in the EC (Constantinescu, 1991a, p. 439). The reason for that change is that the EC, with or without treaty amendments, has entered many new policy fields during the last two decades. In addition, treaty amendments have broadened the scope of majority decisions, and at the same time the political principle enshrined in the so-called Luxembourg accords of 1966, namely that unanimity must be sought where a Member state pleads its vital interests to be affected, apparently has fallen into desuetude. Thus, the question becomes more serious: what kinds of policy field and decision should be dealt with by the Community and which should be retained at the level of the Member states. With this kind of problem or even controversy, it is natural that the idea of subsidiarity reappear (Constantinescu, 1991a, p.439 *et seq.* 1991b, p. 561 *et seq.*; Schmidhuber and Hitzler, 1992, p. 720 *et seq.*; Hitzler, 1991, p. 13 *et seq.*).

Special problems in this respect have come up in the field of environmental policy. It was argued that environmental standards adopted by the EC were only the lowest common denominator and should thus not prevent Member states from taking more stringent measures to protect their environment (Gündling, 1988, p. 28 *et seq.*). To state it a little differently, although some protection was needed under EC law, to take environmentally lazy states aboard the environmental ship, better protection could be, should be and was provided by the environmentally progressive Member states. Whether they were always as advanced as they claimed to be is another question, but this is how the issue was perceived by the relevant actors and thus the political controversy was real.

As a result, certain clauses to protect the Member states' interest in taking more severe and strict environmental measures were inserted into the EC treaty when it was amended in order to facilitate the creation of the single market and to introduce environmental protection as a field of Community policy. Two articles, Article 100a, paragraph 4 (under very restrictive conditions) and Article 130r, provide in different ways for more stringent national environmental protection rules. In addition, the powers of the Community in the field of environmental policy are somewhat limited by the following provision which, at least at first glance, seems to be a subsidiarity clause:

> The Community shall take action relating to the environment to the extent to which the objectives referred to in para. 1 (of Art. 130r) can be attained better at Community level than at the level of the individual Member states...

The meaning of this so-called 'better' clause is, however, somewhat controversial. Some authors do not consider this provision to be a limitation on Community powers, but rather a political perspective to seek the best level of action for measures of environmental protection (Krämer, 1991, p. 3982 *et seq.*[1]). It is not our purpose to discuss this in greater detail. What is important to us, however, is the fact that the provision at least invites some reflection on the appropriate level of decision-making in environmental matters. It clearly appears from the existing literature in relation to Article 130r of the EC treaty, that there are very few, if any, general rules as to what kinds of environmental goal may be better attained at the Community level.

The question of the limitation of Community powers and the insertion of a subsidiarity clause for that purpose was subject to a heated debate in the negotiations leading to the Maastricht Treaty on European Union. Certain Member states of the Community, and in particular the Member states of the Federal Republic of Germany, strongly put forward the case for a subsidiarity clause (Hochbaum, 1992, p. 290; Eiselstein, 1991, p. 21). The result is a provision which in certain respects resembles Article 130r, paragraph 4, but which makes it very clear that it is to be understood as a limitation of Community powers. Article 3b of what is now the Treaty Establishing the European Community reads as follows:

- The Community shall act within the limits of the powers conferred upon it by this Treaty and the objectives assigned to it therein.

- In areas which do not fall within its exclusive competence, the Community shall take action in accordance with the principle of subsidiarity, only if and in so far as the objectives of the proposed action cannot be sufficiently achieved by the Member states and can therefore by reason of the scale or effects of those action be better achieved by the Community.

- Any action by the Community shall not go beyond what is necessary to achieve the objectives of this treaty.

This provision makes the requirements for justification of Community action much more stringent than Article 130r. It must be established that specific policy goals cannot be attained by action at the level of Member states. In the fields of environmental policy as in others, the article calls for more reflection on what kinds of environmental measures cannot adequately be taken at the national level. That reflection has only just begun, and it is too early to expect any general rules to have emerged.

THE APPROPRIATE LEVEL OF DECISION-MAKING IN ENVIRONMENTAL POLICY

At first glance, it might appear somewhat awkward to discuss the development of international environmental law in the light of the Subsidiarity Principle, i.e. with a view to giving the preference to lower levels of government, in particular to national instead of international regulation. Is our problem that we have so far been unable to create enough international rules or that we have too many of them? If one looks into the development of federal systems and of the EC, which have just been presented, where the rediscovery of subsidiarity is a recent phenomenon, it appears that this adherence to the Subsidiarity Principle is a sign of the maturity in the system. It shows a differentiated approach to the question of the level of decision-making and tries to find the right level by using rational criteria. In this sense

> subsidiarity is part of the movement to rationalise public administration, as it should contribute to finding a new space-related localization of powers and a new appropriate distribution of powers between different orders of the political and administrative organization, which may provide a clear answer to the question of who does what... (Constantinescu, 1991a, p. 442, author's translation).

This kind of rationalization of regulatory approaches is also necessary as far as international environmental law is concerned. This part of international law has so far developed in a haphazard, erratic and often irrational way. In the following lines we will try to take a few tentative steps towards developing a theory of the appropriate level of decision-making in environmental policy, and the desirable division of tasks between national and international regulation.

The fact that the environment of the globe is indivisible seems to suggest that any environmental problem must be dealt with at a global level, but this is far from being true. The protection of the atmosphere is certainly a global problem, but it could well be that the self-interest of each and every state would suffice to induce all states to take appropriate measures. Experience shows, however, that this is not the case. Within the European Communities, there are several cases where it is quite clear that without Community action, certain Member states would not have taken the measures deemed necessary for the protection of the environment (Krämer, 1991, p. 3986). The same is probably true for international rules elaborated within the framework of the United Nations Economic Commission for Europe. It thus appears that international regulation is an important means of overcoming political obstacles to good environmental policy which may exist at the national level in some states. It is not enough to rely on the states' well-informed self-interest if the goal is to preserve the world's environment. This is the basis of treaties that place an upper limit on certain emissions (air and water pollution), but also of the new biodiversity convention. The controversy over a convention for forest conservation shows, however, that there are serious reservations about that concept, which are based on the idea of state sovereignty.

In particular, the self-interest of states cannot be relied upon where it is physically possible for them to export environmental problems; for example, the classic case of the upstream state which pollutes a river without suffering the consequences. Where the sea is involved, every state is an upstream state, and thus pollution of the sea from land-based sources can be prevented only by international regulation.

While it is possible to show that there are many problems where international regulation is necessary to make sure that appropriate measures are taken at all, a search for the appropriate level of decision-making must also address the question of what kinds of measures can better be taken at the national or international level. The fact that some international regulation is needed does not mean that everything has to be regulated at the international level. A good example of the necessary regulatory mix is the 1985 SO_2-Protocol[2] to the 1979 Geneva Convention on Long-range Transboundary Air Pollution. That protocol provides for an overall reduction of SO_2 emissions, but it leaves the states complete freedom as to how to achieve this reduction. It seems possible to achieve agreements on specific overall goals, but it would be much more difficult and in some cases even futile if states tried to agree on specific emission standards for specific kinds of polluting installations (Hohmann, 1992, p. 359).

The same is true for setting water quality standards. Where quality standards are agreed upon for particular water systems, the relevant states can choose how to achieve the quality goal. This can be done by somehow inducing polluting activities to shrink or stop, but the states remain free as to the choice of activities and inducements.[3] That means, as a general principle, that concrete action at a source of pollution could be left to national decision-making, although it means leaving the difficult choices to national implementation of international rules.

These examples partly belong to a second aspect, the concept of shared resources, which requires international regulation. It is obvious that a resource which for physical reasons constitutes a unity, but which is subject to the territorial sovereignty of several states or is situated beyond the limits of national jurisdiction, can only be managed by an international agreement among the states concerned. The decisive practical and political questions are: to what extent management of a resource is needed and which are the states concerned.[4]

Firstly, for many centuries, the resources of the High Seas were not considered to need management and, until very recently, nor did the global atmosphere. The ecological reasons which make resource management necessary in certain cases cannot be analysed in detail here, but if and to what extent management is required, is a case for international regulation. Secondly, the question arises as to which states are concerned. Traditional international regulations of the uses of rivers were to a large extent concerned with navigation. In this perspective, the states concerned are those having navigation interests in a particular river. If an ecological approach is used concerning the regulation of the uses of the river system, then the relevant geographical scope is that of the catchment area of the river system, possibly including neighbouring areas also which for one reason or another have an impact on the catchment area. Regarding sea areas, according to a now well-established international practice, the coastal states of enclosed or semi-enclosed seas are those which are mainly concerned. This is, for example, the basis of UNEP's Regional Seas Programme. But environmental regulations for these areas have an impact on shipping interests of third states, and land-locked states have a keen interest in the preservation and/or exploitation of the resources of the seas. Thus, for many questions an approach which is broader than mere geographic vicinity is appropriate in order to determine the participants in a particular regulating scheme. Sometimes, a link is necessary between regulatory schemes having a different geographic coverage. For instance, some coordination and cooperation is necessary between a treaty system for the protection of the environment of the catchment area of the Danube river (which is being negotiated) and the Convention on the protection of the Black Sea against pollution.[5]

Another important aspect which requires international regulation is a general interest in unrestricted trade. Where states, for environmental and similar reasons, impose requirements on products which are internationally traded, these requirements constitute so-called non-tariff barriers to international trade. Their restraining impact on international trade can be prevented by harmonizing those requirements. This is one of the cases, however, where the question of the lowest common denominator, already mentioned in relation to EC environmental regulation, poses a serious problem. It depends on the kind of economic impact an environmental regulation may have on trade. If the problem is that smaller quantities, meeting the requirements of individual countries, have to be produced for individual country markets and that thus no advantage can be gained from economies of scale, it can be solved by harmonization at any level. To solve this kind of problem of production cost, it does not matter at what level harmonization is achieved. Thus, one is tempted to harmonize at a level which is not optimal from the environmental point of view. This kind of harmonization is somewhat dubious.

There are sometimes serious economic pressures for harmonization at a low level. While certain enterprises with a strong market position are able to meet almost any standard and then benefit from the economies of scale, young or aging industries may not have the capacity to meet those standards. Environmental standards could be used to exclude those industries from the market.

Furthermore, particular ecological conditions may require standards which are not necessary in other areas. In this case, harmonization at the very strict level required for a particularly vulnerable area would be uneconomic and unnecessary; for example, California standards for automobile exhaust gases, which are more stringent than in other parts of the United States.

Another economic consideration which might suggest regulatory action at the international level is the regulation of competition. It is well known that environmental standards applicable to industrial production facilities may increase production costs and thus affect the competitive position of the enterprise in question. It is, thus, often argued that a harmonization of environmental standards for production facilities is also needed in order to avoid environmental dumping or a distortion of competition. This was a basis for early action of the EC in the field of environmental policy based on Article 100 of the EC Treaty, that is to say before the introduction of Article 100a and the chapter on environmental policy by the Single European Act. Where this argument is used to claim lower environmental standards or to oppose stricter environmental standards, some caution is necessary. The attraction of low environmental standards for industrial investment is often overestimated. In some cases, the availability of free space, and maybe also of regenerative capacity of the environment, is a natural advantage of certain locations which must not necessarily be defeated by harmonization. On the other hand, in some countries the availability of open space and regenerative capacity is often grossly exaggerated by politicians who want to attract investment. Thus, the need to harmonize environmental standards for production facilities in order to avoid distortion of competition is a highly complex question.

Having developed some considerations requiring regulation at the international level, one can turn to lower levels. Some elements of environmental policy require decentralized decision-making, which means decision-making at the national or even the subnational level. It is a truism that environmental protection depends on action at the source of pollution or degradation. Enforcement is more a matter for lower levels of government. There is not and will not be any international environmental police force having direct enforcement functions. In the internal organization of states, direct enforcement measures are, to a great extent, at least in larger states, a matter of local decision-making. On the other hand, one cannot entirely rely on local enforcement decisions. All kinds of considerations in local politics, some of which are legitimate and some not, necessitate some control of local enforcement action. Similar considerations may apply in respect of the relationship between national and international controls. Most enforcement of international environmental law must be left to states, but there should be some kind of international supervisory mechanism.

A matter which is particularly of local concern and requires local decisions is land-use planning. In many countries, zoning decisions, i.e. decision-making on the actual use of particular pieces of land, are made locally. Those decisions have a great impact on the quality of life and the preservation of the environment. Here again, some control of those decisions is needed at a higher level. That is true particularly with respect to the siting of installations which serve larger areas, but which are not very popular in the immediate vicinity, like waste-disposal installations, but also power plants and transportation infrastructure. If one relies on local decision-making only, the necessary service installations might never be constructed. So, one is again confronted with the necessity of a mix of various kinds of decision to be taken at different levels. An example of this mix is the system of air pollution control in the United States where there are national ambient air standards, i.e. fairly uniform goals throughout the country, but whose implementation is left to the states and where the federal government intervenes only to enforce the standards if the states in question are unable to attain the national goals.

These considerations also have some consequences for the choice to be made between national and international regulations. For the implementation of the Climate Convention signed in Rio, energy saving is an important issue. But the ways and means of achieving these savings depend on national conditions and should be decided at the national level. International efforts to combat desertification or to improve the quality of life in human settlements are being, and should be, undertaken. But the land-use decisions they involve must in the end be made at the national and local levels.

Having explained some of the considerations concerning the appropriate level of decision-making, we can now discuss the final question of how the choice of the appropriate level of decision-making, of which the Subsidiarity Principle is an important element, affects other principles of environmental policy.

THE POLLUTER-PAYS PRINCIPLE AND SUBSIDIARITY

The purpose of the Polluter-Pays Principle is to ensure the internalization of external environmental costs (Dommen, Chapter 1 in this volume) which may be effected in different ways. Where it is effected through emission controls designed to prevent harmful effects on the environment, the cost of which has to be borne by the industry controlled, then all possible external effects must be taken into account when the decision on emission controls is taken. If that means taking into account any effect of the polluting activity likely to occur in another country or beyond the limits of national jurisdiction, this can be achieved by an autonomous national decision of the country of origin. But it may be helpful if some international rule requires those transboundary effects to be taken into account. As a matter of fact, this rule is, as a general principle, part of customary international law,[6] but additional rules to the general customary principle, e.g. concerning environmental impact assessment, are desirable. While the principle itself is undisputed, its practical application is often controversial, both as a matter of law and of fact. The kind of physical impact which is caused by an activity may be debated. The dispute over acid precipitation and its actual effect on plants and aquatic life is a case in point. But even where the physical processes of transboundary environmental impacts are known, their evaluation in terms of acceptable risk (this is not a factual, but a political and/or legal evaluation) may be highly controversial. A good example is the acceptability of the risk involved in the peaceful uses of nuclear energy, about which political judgement still differs among countries. After the Chernobyl accident, when radioactive clouds spread over Europe, every country had a different idea of what actually constituted a damage (or to put it in practical terms, what kinds of irradiated food were edible, the country of origin, of course, trying to define 'damage' in a very narrow manner). As these differences may lead to serious international disputes, international standards are desirable.

Another way to implement PPP is through tort liability. Here again, the traditional approach is to leave that to autonomous national decision, rules on jurisdiction and conflict of laws being sufficient in most situations to facilitate transboundary actions. In the EC countries, only the jurisdictional aspect of the problem has so far been addressed by international rules.[7] It has been suggested, however, that other questions relating to transboundary liability for environmental damage should be dealt with by international regulation, especially where that liability goes beyond traditional tort liability. (On recent developments, see Hafner, 1991, p. 91 *et seq.*). International regulation should follow the pattern set by recent national developments concerning product liability and responsibility for environmental damages.

THE USER-PAYS PRINCIPLE AND SUBSIDIARITY

As with PPP, whether implementation of UPP can be achieved only with some kind of higher level, i.e. international regulation, depends on the ways and means in which UPP is implemented. Where environmental costs are indeed reflected in the prices of goods and services which are traded internationally, implementation of UPP can be left to the market mechanism. But this is not necessarily the case. Where a commodity is produced at high environmental cost (for example, mining processes from which heavy metals pollute rivers) and where the producer's market position is weak, the market cannot be relied upon to achieve the desired result that these costs be paid by the 'user', i.e. the buyer of those commodities. Some kind of regulation is necessary to obtain the desirable distribution of financial burdens.

Furthermore, there are cases of an actual transfer from a user to another entity or person behaving in an environmentally desirable way (for example, transfers from water users to farmers who refrain from using chemical fertilizers in order to protect the groundwater against pollution). In some cases of this kind an international regulatory framework to organize these transfers may be appropriate.

THE PRECAUTIONARY PRINCIPLE AND SUBSIDIARITY

As in the case of PPP and UPP, the implementation of the Precautionary Principle (Chisholm and Clarke, Chapter 7 in this volume)may be achieved in different ways with different kinds of regulation, if any. In relation to polluting installations, regulation based on PP is costly and thus affects the competitive position of the enterprise which is subject to these environmental conditions. Thus, the issue of international harmonization is raised again. It is an area where some kind of harmonization between major competitors would make sense. This issue is now being discussed in the EC: whether drastic measures to reduce CO_2 emissions could or should be taken regardless of the fact that there has been no agreement yet on such matters between the EC, the United States and Japan. International regulation would be helpful in this respect. It would not require global harmonization, but at least some harmonization between the major competing industrial powers which are most seriously affected.

SUSTAINABLE DEVELOPMENT AND SUBSIDIARITY

The Subsidiarity Principle is related to sustainable development in many respects. One of the greatest mischiefs of past development policy has been mega-projects which have no actual roots in the environment where they happened to be planned by a centralized bureaucracy or, perhaps even worse, by a foreign enterprise. It is arguable that development would be better achieved by fostering smaller projects involving the self-interest and self-help of the local people. This is, indeed, a form of subsidiarity but only an example of the more general fundamental question of overcoming the centre–periphery imbalance in developing countries. But whether this can be done by simply giving more powers to local governments and organizations or whether this does not rather require some kind of centrally-organized redistribution processes is a different and difficult problem.

As to the choice between the national and international levels of decision-making, it must be stressed that many international instruments proclaiming their adherence to the principle of sustainable development are reluctant to make national decisions as to how sustainable development is to be achieved a matter of international regulation (Bothe, 1991b, p. 63 *et seq.*). The recent controversy, which will probably continue, on international norms for the preservation of forests is an example of the emphasis many developing countries place in this respect on the principle of national sovereignty. While some developing countries (or at least some political forces in these countries) stress the role of forests, mainly tropical rain forests, in affecting the world climate and as a treasure of biodiversity (which makes their preservation a matter of international concern), the countries where these forests are situated (or certain important political forces in those countries) regard them as a resource of a local character which can legitimately be used for timber extraction or be converted to other uses (agriculture, mining, hydroelectric power generation) to increase the income of the population. Although sustainability (i.e. the enlightened self-interest of the forest countries) means restraints on those latter uses it still does not make forest preservation a matter of concern for others.

Insistence on national sovereignty is to a certain extent legitimate. It would be inappropriate if decisions on sustainable development were taken in international forums and not by the people concerned. As experience shows, decisions relating to sustainability rather than to development, which are imposed by international agencies, are difficult for some countries to accept and thus difficult to implement. In this connection subsidiarity is probably a better word for sovereignty. It has an important role to play in relation to sustainable development. However, as already discussed in connection with many other environmental problems, some kind of control and possible corrective action regarding local decisions are appropriate and necessary. There are already some trends to internationalize decisions relating to sustainable development, thus diminishing the role of the Subsidiarity Principle.

In respect of the preservation of the environment, we are witnessing a development which took place (and was very controversial) in relation to human rights, i.e. that there are basic international values which the international community must protect. National sovereignty or subsidiarity must not be used as a shield against these legitimate common concerns.

SUMMARY AND CONCLUSIONS

The Subsidiarity Principle, based on philosophical, political and practical considerations, means a preference for lower-level decision-making. It can be applied between local and state governments, between members of a federation and the federation, or between national and international regulation. Political choices relating to the level of decision-making have varied throughout history according to the changing concepts of state functions. Recently, the approach to these questions has become more differentiated, reversing earlier trends towards centralization and rediscovering subsidiarity.

Within the European Community, discussions on subsidiarity have been triggered by the recent growth of Community powers. It is related to a controversy concerning the role of EC harmonization in the field of the environment and the need, which is felt in certain states, for more stringent national standards. One of the first results of this debate was the inclusion of a clause in the Single European Act which requires Community action for the protection of the environment only where environmental policy goals can be better attained at the Community level than at the level of the individual states. The Maastricht treaty expressly refers to subsidiarity and limits Community powers to those cases where particular objectives can be better attained at the Community level. This requires more reflection on the appropriate level of decision-making. Rational criteria must be found to justify the choices to be made.

More reflection is also needed regarding the choice between national and international regulation. International environmental law has developed so far in a somewhat haphazard way. The choice between national and international decision-making relating to the environment should also be based on rational criteria.

The following reasons favour international regulation:

• the need to induce reluctant states to adopt more stringent, or any, measures;

- the need to manage resources situated within several states or in areas beyond the limits of national jurisdiction;
- the need to avoid non-tariff barriers to trade;
- the need, if any, to avoid distortions of competition due to different environmental costs.

The following considerations favour national (or even subnational) decisions:

- the greater potential of enforcement action taken close to the source of a problem;
- the need to take land-use decisions locally and with the participation of those concerned;
- acceptability of decisions.

As a rule, these criteria do not mean that a particular subject matter as a whole should be assigned to a particular level of decision-making. As a rule, a regulatory mix is required to facilitate a sensible division of functions and concertation between various levels of decision-making.

Other principles of environmental policy also influence the choice of the level of decision-making. Both the Polluter-Pays Principle and the User-Pays Principle should ensure that certain costs that occur elsewhere are borne by a particular actor (the user or the polluter). If these costs occur in other states, it cannot be assumed that the redistribution takes place automatically and thus international rules are needed to achieve the desired result. The application of the Precautionary Principle may also intend to take into account environmental effects occurring outside the country where a decision is made. This might also favour some kind of international regulation. Decisions concerning sustainable development are often regarded as a sovereign decision of the country in question. But many questions of sustainability are also a matter of common concern for mankind. Sovereignty or subsidiarity should not be used to shield states against these legitimate common concerns.

NOTES

1 A slightly different view is taken by Grabitz (marginal note 71 *et seq.*), but he rejects the view that the 'better' clause is to be understood as a subsidiarity clause.
2 Protocol to the 1979 Convention on Long-range Transboundary Air Pollution on the Reduction of Sulphur Emissions or their Transboundary Fluxes by at least 30 per cent, Helsinki, 8 July 1985.
3 This is, for instance, the sense of the so-called Rhine Action Plan adopted in 1987, which only sets certain quality goals.
4 Draft Principles of Conduct in the Field of the Environment fo the Guidance of States in the Conservation and Harmonious Utilization of Natural Resources Shared by two or more States, 17 International Legal Materials 1091 (1978).

5 That Convention was adopted at a conference held in Bucharest on 21 April 1992.
6 This was, in particular, recognized by the Lac Lanoux arbitration (see Rauschning, 1981, p. 167).
7 European Convention on Jurisdiction and Enforcement of Judgements in Civil and Commercial Matters, as amended, 18 ILM 21 (1979).

ANNEX 1

THE POLLUTER-PAYS PRINCIPLE: DEFINITIONS AND RECOMMENDATIONS[1]

RECOMMENDATION OF THE COUNCIL

ON GUIDING PRINCIPLES CONCERNING INTERNATIONAL

ECONOMIC ASPECTS OF ENVIRONMENTAL POLICIES
(Adopted by the Council at its 293rd Meeting on 26th May, 1972)

The Council,

Having regard to Article 5(b) of the Convention on the Organisation for Economic Co-operation and Development of 14th December, 1960;

Having regard to the Resolution of the Council of 22nd July, 1970 Establishing an Environment Committee;

Having regarding to the Report by the Environment Committee on Guiding Principles Concerning the International Economic Aspects of Environmental Policies;

Having regard to the views expressed by interested committees;

Having regard to the Note by the Secretary-General;

I. RECOMMENDS that the Governments of Member countries should, in determining environmental control policies and measures, observe the 'Guiding Principles Concerning the International Economic Aspects of Environmental Policies' set forth in the Annex to this Recommendation.

II. INSTRUCTS the Environment Committee to review as it deems appropriate the implementation of this Recommendation.

III. INSTRUCTS the Environment Committee to recommend as soon as

possible the adoption of appropriate mechanisms for notification and/or consultation or some other appropriate form of action.
Annex

GUIDING PRINCIPLES CONCERNING THE INTERNATIONAL ECONOMIC ASPECTS OF ENVIRONMENTAL POLICIES

Introduction

1. The guiding principles described below concern mainly the international aspects of environmental policies with particular reference to their economic and trade implications. These principles do not cover for instance, the particular problems which may arise during the transitional periods following the implementation of the principles, instruments for the implementation of the so-called 'Polluter-Pays Principle', exceptions to this principle, trans-frontier pollution, or possible problems related to developing countries.

A. GUIDING PRINCIPLES

a) Cost Allocation: the Polluter-Pays Principle

2. Environmental resources are in general limited and their use in production and consumption activities may lead to their deterioration. When the cost of this deterioration is not adequately taken into account in the price system, the market fails to reflect the scarcity of such resources both at the national and international levels. Public measures are thus necessary to reduce pollution and to reach a better allocation of resources by ensuring that prices of goods depending on the quality and/or quantity of environmental resources reflect more closely their relative scarcity and that economic agents concerned react accordingly.

3. In many circumstances, in order to ensure that the environment is in an acceptable state, the reduction of pollution beyond a certain level will not be practical or even necessary in view of the costs involved.

4. The principle to be used for allocating costs of pollution prevention and control measures to encourage rational use of scarce environmental resources and to avoid distortions in international trade and investment is the so-called 'Polluter-Pays Principle'. The Principle means that the polluter should bear the expenses of carrying out the above-mentioned measures decided by public

authorities to ensure that the environment is in an acceptable state. In other words, the cost of these measures should be reflected in the cost of goods and services which cause pollution in production and/or consumption. Such measures should not be accompanied by subsidies that would create significant distortions in international trade and investment.

5. This Principle should be an objective of Member countries; however, there may be exceptions or special arrangements, particularly for the transitional periods, provided that they do not lead to significant distortions in international trade and investment.

b) Environmental Standards

6. Differing national environmental policies, for example with regard to the tolerable amount of pollution and to quality and emission standards, are justified by a variety of factors including, among other things, different pollution assimilative capacities of the environment in its present state, different social objectives and priorities attached to environmental protection and different degrees of industrialization and population density.

7. In view of this, a very high degree of harmonization of environmental policies which would be otherwise desirable may be difficult to achieve in practice; however it is desirable to strive towards more stringent standards in order to strengthen environmental protection, particularly in cases where less stringent standards would not be fully justified by the above-mentioned factors.

8. Where valid reasons for differences do not exist, Governments should seek harmonization of environmental policies, for instance with respect to timing and the general scope of regulation for particular industries to avoid the unjustified disruption of international trade patterns and of the international allocation of resources which may arise from diversity of national environmental standards.

9. Measures taken to protect the environment should be framed, as far as possible, in such a manner as to avoid the creation of non-tariff barriers to trade.

10. Where products are traded internationally and where there could be significant obstacles to trade, Governments should seek common standards for polluting products and agree on the timing and general scope of regulations for particular products.

c) National Treatment and Non-Discrimination

11. In conformity with the provisions of the GATT, measures taken within an environmental policy regarding polluting products should be applied in accordance with the principle of national treatment (i.e. identical treatment for imported products and similar domestic products) and with the principle of non-discrimination (identical treatment for imported products regardless of their national origin).

d) Procedures of Control

12. It is highly desirable to define in common, as rapidly as possible, procedures for checking conformity to product standards established for the purpose of environmental control. Procedures for checking conformity to standards should be mutually agreed so as to be applied by an exporting country to the satisfaction of the importing country.

e) Compensating Import Levies and Export Rebates

13. In accordance with the provisions of the GATT, differences in environmental policies should not lead to the introduction of compensating import levies or export rebates, or measures having an equivalent effect, designed to offset the consequences of these differences on prices. Effective implementation of the guiding principles set forth herewith will make it unnecessary and undesirable to resort to such measures.

B. CONSULTATIONS

14. Consultations on the above-mentioned principles should be pursued. In connection with the application of these guiding principles, a specific mechanism of consultation and/or notification, or some other appropriate form of action, should be determined as soon as possible, taking into account the work done by other international organizations.

NOTE ON THE IMPLEMENTATION OF THE POLLUTER-PAYS PRINCIPLE

Introduction

Within the framework of the 'Guiding Principles concerning International Economic Aspects of Environmental Policies', the Polluter-Pays Principle contributes to the avoidance of distortions in international trade and investment.

This paper is intended to offer clarifications for the practical implementation of the Polluter-Pays principle. It should however be noted that:

– such implementation must be considered in connection with that of the other parts of the Guiding Principles;

– the dynamic aspects of the implementation of the Polluter-Pays Principle have not been fully considered here.

A. DEFINITION

1. The Polluter-Pays Principle (applying to transitional periods with possible exceptions and in the long term) implies that in general it is for the polluter to meet the costs of pollution control and prevention measures, irrespective of whether these costs are incurred as the result of the imposition of some charge on pollution emission, or are debited through some other suitable economic mechanism, or are in response to some direct regulation leading to some enforced reduction in pollution.

2. The Polluter-Pays Principle, as defined in paragraph 4 of the 'Guiding Principles', states that the polluter should bear the expenses of preventing and controlling pollution 'to ensure that the environment is in an acceptable state'. The notion of an 'acceptable state' decided by public authorities, implies that through a collective choice and with respect to the limited information available, the advantage of a further reduction in the residual social damage involved is considered as being smaller than the social cost of further prevention and control. In fact, the Polluter-Pays Principle is no more than an efficiency principle for allocating costs and does not involve bringing pollution down to an optimum level of any type, although it does not exclude the possibility of doing so.

3. To reach a better allocation of resources in line with paragraph 2 of the Guiding Principles, it is desirable that the private costs of goods and services should reflect the relative scarcity of environmental resources used in their production. If this is the case, consumers and producers would adjust themselves to the total social costs for the goods and services they are buying and selling. The Polluter-Pays Principle is a means of moving towards this end. From the point of view of conformity with the Polluter-Pays Principle, it does not matter whether the polluter passes on to his prices some or all of the environment costs or absorbs them.

B. INSTRUMENTS FOR APPLYING THE POLLUTER-PAYS PRINCIPLE

4. The Polluter-Pays Principle may be implemented by various means ranging from process and product standards, individual regulation and prohibitions to levying various kinds of pollution charges. Two or more of these instruments can be used together. The choice of instruments is particularly important as the effectiveness of a policy depends on it. This choice can only be made by public authorities at central or regional level, in the light of a number of factors such as the amount of information required for the efficient use of these various instruments, their administrative cost, etc.

5. Direct regulations could be of exceptional value in achieving immediate or speedy pollution reduction needed to safeguard public health or abate unacceptable nuisance. They would also be more appropriate in cases where the kind of pollutant or the structure of the group of polluters (because of their number or of their composition) make the charge system less effective.

6. In other cases, pollution prevention and control measures may achieve a desired improvement of the quality of the environment to least social costs when they are based on the levying of charges. When charges are applied they should be put in the framework of a comprehensive policy. Such a policy will make explicit the function of charges in relation to environmental policy objectives and to other instruments. When a charge is levied, it induces polluters to treat their effluents as long as the treatment costs remain lower than the amount of the charge they would otherwise be compelled to pay in the absence of pollution abatement. A charging policy may thus achieve an objective at least social cost to society as it would induce each of these polluters to abate pollution to the point where they each incur the same additional cost for the same reduction of pollution emission.

Another advantage of charges is that they can provide a continuing incentive for improved pollution abatement.

Charges may also be levied for example by regional bodies as a means of achieving an efficient cost allocation. In such a system some firms may treat more waste and this service can be financed through the charges levied. Charges may also be used in order to cover the costs of collective waste treatment plants. These charges will correspond to a purchase of services financed by all the polluters who are using the services and will thus be in line with the Polluter-Pays Principle.

C. EXCEPTIONS TO THE POLLUTER-PAYS PRINCIPLE

7. An environmental policy will normally be put into effect gradually. In certain circumstances such as a speedy or a sudden and very extensive implementation of environmental policy, environmental improvements may be helped and even speeded up if existing polluters are given aid in their initial or transitional efforts to reduce their emissions. Aid payments for such purposes will only be a valid exception to the Polluter-pays Principle if they form part of transitional arrangements whose duration has been laid down in advance and do not lead to significant distortions in international trade and investment. Such transitional arrangements can also include a time-table for progressively tightening up emission standards and raising the scale of charges to the levels required to reach the quality targets.

8. Exceptions to the Polluter-Pays Principle may also be justified when steps to protect the environment would jeopardize the social and economic policy objectives of a country or region. This would be the case, for example, when the additional expenditure incurred by polluting industries would result in holding back regional development or adversely affecting the labour market. However, in the spirit of the general principle approved, it is recommended that such exceptions are kept at the level and for the time strictly necessary to reach the specific socio-economic objectives. Aid to promote research and development in line with other aspects of government policy is not inconsistent with the Polluter-Pays Principle.

**RECOMMENDATION OF THE COUNCIL
ON THE IMPLEMENTATION OF THE
POLLUTER-PAYS PRINCIPLE**

(Adopted by the Council at its 372nd Meeting on 14 November, 1974)

The Council,

Having regard to Article 5(b) of the Convention on the Organisation for Economic Co-operation and Development of 14th December, 1960;

Having regard to the provisions of the General Agreement on Tariffs and Trade;

Having regard to the Recommendation of the Council of 26th May, 1972 on Guiding Principles Concerning International Economic Aspects of Environmental Policies;

Having regard to the Note by the Environment Committee on Implementation of the Polluter-Pays Principle;

Having regard to the possibility, approved by the Council, of holding informal consultations on the Guiding Principles within the OECD;

On the proposal of the Environment Committee;

I. REAFFIRMS that:

1.   The Polluter-Pays Principle constitutes for Member countries a fundamental principle for allocating costs of pollution prevention and control measures introduced by the public authorities in Member countries.
2.   The Polluter-Pays Principle, as defined by the Guiding Principles concerning International Economic Aspects of Environmental Policies, which take account of particular problems possibly arising for developing countries, means that the polluter should bear the expenses of carrying out the measures, as specified in the previous paragraph, to ensure that the environment is in an acceptable state. In other words, the cost of these measures should be reflected in the cost of goods and services which cause pollution in production and/or consumption.
3.   Uniform application of this principle, through the adoption of a

common basis for Member countries' environmental policies, would encourage the rational use and the better allocation of scarce environmental resources and prevent the appearance of distortions in international trade and investment.

II. NOTES that:

1. There is a close relationship between a country's environmental policy and its overall socio-economic policy;

2. In exceptional circumstances, such as the rapid implementation of a compelling and especially stringent pollution control regime, socio-economic problems may develop of such significance as to justify consideration of the granting of governmental assistance if the environmental policy objectives of a Member country are to be realized within a prescribed and specified time;

3. Aid given for the purpose of stimulating experimentation with new pollution-control technologies and development of new pollution-abatement equipment is not necessarily incompatible with the Polluter-Pays Principle;

4. Where measures taken to promote a country's specific socio-economic objectives, such as the reduction of serious inter-regional imbalances, would have the incidental effect of constituting aid for pollution-control purposes, the granting of such aid would not be inconsistent with the Polluter-Pays Principle.

III. RECOMMENDS that:

1. Member countries continue to collaborate and work closely together in striving for uniform observance of the Polluter-Pays Principle, and therefore that as a general rule they should not assist the polluters in bearing the costs of pollution control whether by means of subsidies, tax advantages or other measures;

2. The granting of any such assistance for pollution control be strictly limited, and in particular comply with every one of the following conditions:

a) it should be selective and restricted to those parts of the economy, such as industries, areas or plants, where severe difficulties would otherwise occur;

b) it should be limited to well-defined transitional periods, laid down in advance and adapted to the specific socio-economic problems associated with the implementation of a country's environmental programme;

c) it should not create significant distortions in international trade and investment;

3. That if a Member country, in cases of exceptional difficulty, gives assistance to new plants, the conditions be even stricter than those applicable to existing plants and that criteria on which to base this differentiation be developed;

4. In accordance with appropriate procedures to be worked out, all systems to provide assistance be notified to Member countries through the OECD Secretariat. Wherever practicable these notifications would occur prior to implementation of such systems;

5. Regardless of whether notification has taken place, consultations, as mentioned in the Guiding Principles, on the implementation of such systems, will take place at the request of any Member State.

IV. INVITES the Environment Committee to report to the Council on action taken pursuant to this Recommendation.

NOTES

1   OECD 1975.

ANNEX II

NATURAL RESOURCE MANAGEMENT AND THE USER-PAYS PRINCIPLE

This paper was prepared by the OECD Secretariat for 'the Group of Economic Experts', one of the subsidiary bodies of the Environment Committee. The principles of Resource Pricing in the environmental context were originally developed as the 'User-Pays Principle' by another subsidiary body, the Group on Natural Resource Management. It was recognized by both groups that there were some overlaps between the two set of principles, Polluter-Pays (PPP) and User-Pays (UPP), and this paper explores some of these overlaps. Finally it was decided by the Groups that, in order to avoid misunderstandings and conflicts, the term 'Resource Pricing' should be used rather than 'User-Pays Principle'.

1. EFFICIENT NATURAL RESOURCE MANAGEMENT

The basic tenet of the natural resource management programme is that efficient natural resource management is tantamount to good environmental management. This was not self-evident when the Committee first discussed this programme. Efficient natural resource management requires careful definition so that resource costs and prices reflect the costs of the external effects associated with exploiting, transforming and using natural resources together with the costs of foregone, future uses of depleted resources, and thereby ensuring efficient use of these resources. The internalisation of costs can be achieved through regulations and/or economic instruments and it is anticipated that these costs will ultimately be passed on, in part, to consumers.

The Environment Committee, in setting up the programme, also stressed the point that environmental management conducted through natural resource management has an automatic anticipatory policy built into the system. Efficient natural resource management policies, by anticipating environmental impacts, reduce environmental damage and consequently reduce pollution prevention and control costs. For example, if water is priced at full cost, including external costs, water will be used more efficiently, particularly in industry and agriculture, and consequently water use and pollution will be reduced.

The nature of many natural resources, such as common property, the public good nature of certain resource flows and external diseconomies cause market imperfections when dealing with these goods and provide the primary rationale for natural resource and environmental policies.

In confronting common property or externality problems, policy makers have usually adopted a rule making enforcement policy strategy. Public regulatory bodies have been designed to control the behaviour of users of the resource. Rule setting, behaviour monitoring and rule enforcement have been the standard practice of control. An example is the use of permits, which are generally heavily regulated and are usually allocated on criteria other than efficiency in resource use.

The result of such practices is that users with access to the resource are not charged a price that represents its full economic value. The failure of policy to rely on economic values in controlling resource use also create incentives for resource users to adopt uneconomic and environmentally degrading practices.

As a general policy goal, countries should manage renewable resources on a sustainable basis in a way that will promote economic growth and in a manner that will economise on the administrative and procedural dimensions of their management. Additionally, such management is assumed to be with full regard for environmental quality and for quality of human life.

In general, in most OECD countries, economic strategies designed to achieve the optimal sustainable output level and to equate marginal private and social costs for the use of natural resources have not been adopted. This in part, has been due to the absence of institutional arrangements that stimulate and support objective evaluations of existing and proposed policy and to ensure that economic analyses of policy alternatives are utilised in policy deliberations.

2.   USER-PAYS PRINCIPLE

There is, therefore, a need to implement an economic policy for the management of natural resources that ties the beneficiaries of the use of a resource to the associated costs.

The adoption of the User-Pays Principle (UPP) for the allocation and charging for resource use would be a major factor in reducing resource use conflicts, minimising environmental and social impacts and improving resource use efficiency.

The UPP defines that all resource users should pay for the full long-run marginal social cost of the use of a resource and related services, including any associated treatment costs.

The User-Pays Principle, therefore, encompasses the Polluter-Pays Principle, which was pioneered by the Environment Committee and provides guidance for cost allocation at the *disposal end of natural resources use*. While the Polluter-Pays principle has been used as the guiding principle for the major polluting resources management, the User-Pays Principle is applied both when resources are being consumed and when they are *discharged*. Consequently, the User-Pays Principle, *which is basically the underlying principle of the economies of all OECD countries*, is now proposed to apply as an overall guiding principle to the use of all natural resources such as water (including marine resources) land and forests.

3.   WHO IS THE USER

Resource users can be generally categorised into two types:– Consumptive users and amenity users. Consumptive users of a resource can be categorised as being of three particular types:

(i)   those who physically use the resource volumetrically;
(ii) those who use the absorption capacity of the resource for disposal of waste and by-products of their activities; and
(iii) those who use a resource for both purposes.

For example, in the case of water resources, water is taken volumetrically for activities such as domestic water supply, irrigation and industry. In turn, the absorption capacity of a water resource is influenced by the disposal of residual or waste water resources through either direct discharge or run-off into surface waters or by percolation into groundwaters.

From an environmental viewpoint this can cause problems:

(i)   when the water which returns to the system is of a lower quality from that which it was acquired; or
(ii) when the water which returns to the system is of a lower quality than that of the receiving system.

Amenity users are characterized by the fact that they neither physically consume nor necessarily pollute natural resources. Amenity users can be both active and passive in their use of natural resources. In the case of water resources, amenity users include active and passive recreation, navigation and existence value.

Amenity users can also exceed the sustainable limits of a resource. For example, overcrowding or an incompatible mix of recreational uses.

4. WHAT SHOULD BE PAID

There are market incentives and sanctions to modify resource use. Correct pricing is about selecting the proper shadow prices for natural resources that will properly reflect their marginal social (as opposed to private/individual) value. The UPP proposes that the price for the use of a resource should be the full long-run marginal social cost of using that resource including the external costs associated with its development and any resultant pollution prevention and control activities. In such a system the price reflects the environmental costs to the community of satisfying marginal demands. These environmental costs include quantitative and qualitative resource depletion costs, damage costs and the various capital and operating resource costs. Thus, for example, the price of the last litre of water to be used or disposed of would be equal to the true marginal cost of providing that water service. In this way, the marginal value of the litre abstracted, consumed or disposed of in each use could be the same, the supply system would be used at its economic optimum rate; and, in the long-run, the supply system would be constructed and maintained at the optimal economic scale.

For consumptive uses, such as those found in the household, industrial and agricultural sectors, the price charged for water and other resources, therefore, should be set at the point of intake.

In addition, by applying the User-Pays Principle, the absorption capacity of water to receive pollutants would never be exceeded. Both surface and groundwater are used as recipients for discharges from water users and if as the consequence of these discharges, the water has to be treated, the discharger (user) should have to pay for the costs of treatment. These costs are quite distinct from the cost of water intake, even though in some cases the quantity of intake is used as a proxy for charging for the discharge. The concept that users should also have to pay for the cost of water treatment is now widely accepted in the case of the public sewerage treatment, but has not been generally adopted in other areas. The same principle, however, should also apply to discharges into surface and groundwater by all polluters, especially industry and agriculture. These costs should not be paid by subsequent users who need to treat water before they use it, nor those who incur increased costs as a result of previously inappropriate uses, nor general taxpayers.

Clearly there are difficulties in identifying some polluters, particularly when they are many, and when the sources are diffuse. In some cases the pollution has been caused in the past by people who may no longer be in a position to pay and to pass the costs on to consumers. Nevertheless, it is clear from the Polluter-Pays Principle that the cost of pollution prevention and control should be borne by the discharger (polluter).

Concerning charges for the discharge of polluted water, the discharger normally would be liable only for the cost of clean-up or treatment. These could include charges for the treatment of groundwater for nitrate pollution and also the cost of constructing sediment traps to stop soil erosion from farmland reaching rivers. It may also be appropriate in some situations to charge now for future treatment of groundwater which may be necessary in ten to fifteen years time. A pollution control programme may also involve simply increasing water charges, especially discharge costs. For example, in certain situations it may be appropriate to raise charges so as to reduce the impact of downstream pollution on the income received by fishermen.

In every sense then, the implementation of pricing for resource use that reflects the full long-run marginal social cost of using the resource, would promote economically efficient and environmentally sustainable use of resources.

5. HOW TO MAKE THE USER-PAYS PRINCIPLE WORK

The requirements of the User-Pays Principle and the attached pricing and charging conditions are very stringent and can be made into a self-driving mechanism for integration. These requirements are:

- to calculate the *price* of supply and distribution of a resource on the basis of the capital, operation and maintenance cost of the latest addition to the supply system. This necessitates co-operation between the appropriate administrative agency and the finance ministry;
- to incorporate the *external costs* into the above calculation, requiring an integrated effort between the resource agency, the environment agency and all the other natural resource management agencies;
- to ensure that *price and policy adjustments* are made in as transparent a way as possible to accommodate conditions of practicability and social equity involving close consultation between all levels of government and all consumers; and
- to ensure that *damages* resulting in serious and in some cases irreversible losses affecting future generations are avoided. An integrated management effort amongst development agencies and environment and finance ministries would be required in order that these potential costs be somehow reflected in the price of the resource.

Until recently few cases were known where the User-Pays Principle combined with the appropriate pricing policy has been put into operation. Much of the opposition has come from user groups who at present are enjoying substantial subsidies. Other opposing groups have been the natural resource development agencies themselves who recognised that such new approaches would have an impact on their own operations in two ways:

- more efficient and possibly a reduced volume of resource use will lead, at least in the short-run, to reduced activity on the part of the development (e.g. water resource) agency and consequently perhaps to a smaller budget and loss of power in the bureaucratic hierarchy; and
- closer inter-agency co-operation necessitated through the application of the Principle would lead to some loss of independence and identity, partly *vis-à-vis* other agencies and partly *vis-à-vis* their own constituency; the various consumer groups.

For these reasons governments, both at the central and at the state or provincial levels, have to create by specific actions the conditions for the application of the User-Pays Principle and thereby ensure that this integrating mechanism can come into full force. There are certain minimum conditions to achieve this:

- a requirement, backed by legislation or regulation, that in all natural resource projects the *User-Pays Principle should apply*, setting out also all the requirements for pricing under the Principle;
- *phasing out government grants* for resource projects for which the User-Pays Principle is not being observed and thereby forcing the agency involved to apply the Principle;
- making the payments of general grants to lower levels of government *conditional* on the application of the Principle; and
- making the allocation of loan funds or permission to raise loans by development agencies or lower levels of government *conditional* on the application of the Principle.

It is generally agreed that financing and economic instruments set at an appropriate level can be more effective than regulations on their own. This is particularly true when it comes to the behaviour of a complex bureaucracy as is the case with the management of many natural resources. The proper application of the User-pays Principle could substantially improve the integration of the administrative framework involved in natural resource development and environmental management.

6.   SUMMING UP

It has been demonstrated in another report that the User-Pays Principle can be developed into the basis for efficient water resource management. At the same time the Principle will facilitate and drive further integration of the administrative machinery and thereby again help to achieve economic and environmental objectives.   However, there are a number of impediments to the full implementation of the Principle. Some are technical measurement problems, others concern the equity claims of particular user groups. In addition there is the question of governments embracing the Principle wholeheartedly and their willingness to apply it in face of opposition by their own bureaucracy.

As presented above a set of stringent financial and institutional conditions can be created which would greatly assist the implementation of the User-Pays Principle and thereby better integration.

ACRONYMS

PPP	Polluter-Pays Principle
UPP	User-Pays Principle
PP	Precautionary Principle
SP	Subsidiarity Principle
UNCED	United Nations Conference on Environment and Development
UNCTAD	United Nations Conference on Trade and Development
OECD	Organisation for Economic Cooperation and Development
GATT	General Agreement on Tariffs and Trade
TDP	Transferable Discharge Permits
C and C	Command and Control Policies
SME	Small- and Medium-Scale Enterprises
ECE	European Economic Community
TNC	Transnational Corporations
IDB	Inter-American Development Bank
GDP	Gross Domestic Product
ECLAC	United Nations Economic Commission for Latin America and the Caribbean
UNCTC	United Nations Centre on Transnational Corporations
WRI	World Resources Institute
EGE	Enhanced Greenhouse Effect
GNP	Gross National Product
EUT	Expected Utility Theory
QOV	Quasi-Option Value
EC	European Community
UNEP	United Nations Environment Programme

REFERENCES

Akerlof, G.A. (1991), 'Procrastination and Obedience', *American Economic Review*, May, 81, pp.1-19.

Alfaro, Juan (1989), 'Artículos sobre Saneamiento Básico Ambiental', paper presented the Conference on Organization and Financing of the Seweraget Alfaro to the Conference in Organization and Financing of the Sewerage Services in the Caribbean, IDB, Port of Spain, Trinidad and Tobago, October.

Arrow, K. J. (1979) 'The Property Rights Doctrine and Demand Revelation under Incomplete Information', in *Collected papers of Kenneth J. Arrow*, Vol.4, Harvard University Press, Cambridge, Mass, 1984.

Arrow, K.J. and A.C. Fisher, (1974), 'Environmental Preservation, Uncertainty, and Irreversibility', *Quarterly Journal of Economics*, 88, pp.312-19.

Arrubla Pancar, Jaime Alberto (1991), 'Propuesta de Regulación Ambiental para la Amazonia en Colombia' in Dourado, Maria Cristina (ed.), *Direito Ambiental e a Questao Amazonica*, Asociaçao de Universidades Amazonicas, Brazil.

Asenjo, Rafael (1989), 'Innovative Environmental Legislation in Chile: the case of Chañaral', *Georgetown International Environmental Law Review*, vol. II: issue 2, fall.

Asenjo, Rafael and Santiago Torres, (1991), 'Análisis de Implicancias Económicas de Algunas Decisiones de la Corte Suprema sobre Materias Ambientales', in *Desarrollo y Medio Ambiente*, CIEPLAN, Santiago, Chile.

Ayres, R.U. (1991), 'Comment on, "Global Warming: Economic Policy in the Face of Positive and Negative Spillovers"', in Siebert, H. and Mohr, T. (eds) *Environmental Scarcity: The International Dimension*, pp.213-215.

Barde, J.-P., (1991), 'Economic Instruments for Controlling Persistent Micropollutants: A Comment', pp. 177-182 in: Opschoor, J.B. and Pearce, D.W. (eds.), *Persistent Pollutants*, Kluwer, Dordrecht/Boston/London.

Barrett, S. (1990), *Economic Instruments for Global Climate Change Policy*, Environment Directorate, OECD, Paris.

Baumol, W.J. and W.E. Oates (1988) *The theory of environmental policy*, second edition, Cambridge University Press, Cambridge.

Bergen Ministerial Declaration on Sustainable Development in the ECE Region, held in Bergen, Norway, 16 May 1990.

Bleckmann, Albert and Michael Bothe, (1986), 'General Report on the Theory of Limitations on Human Rights', in de Mestral, A. *et al.* (eds.) *The Limitation of Human Rights in Comparative Constitutional Law*, p.105-112, Y. Blais, Cowansville, Quebec.

Bonus, Holger (1984), *Marktwirtschaftliche Konzepte im Umweltschutz*, Ulmer, Stuttgart,

Boswell, James, *Boswell's life of Johnson*, Entry for 19 September 1779, Oxford University Press, 1953 edition.

Bothe, Michael (1977), *Die Kompetenzstruktur des modernen Bundesstaates in rechtsvergleichender Sicht*, Heymanns, Cologne.

Bothe, Michael (1987), Final Report in International Association of Constitutional Law (ed.), *Federalism and Decentralization*, pp.411-423, Editions Universitaires, Fribourg.

Bothe, Michael (1991), The Constitutional Court of the Federal Republic of Germany and the Powers of the German Länder in Orban, E. (ed.), *Federalism and Supreme Courts*, p.119-136, Bruylant, Brussels; Presses de l'Université de Montréal, Montreal.

Bothe, Michael (1991), 'Internationalization of Natural Resource Management', vol. 2, p.61-66, *Yearbook of International Environmental Law*.

Brañes, Raul (1991), 'Institutional and Legal Aspects of the Environment in Latin America including the participation of Non-Governmental Organizations in Environmental Management', IDB, Washington D.C.

159

160   Fair Principles for Sustainable Development

Buchanan, J.M. and W.C. Stubbeline, (1962) 'Externality,' *Economica N.S.*, pp.29 (1962), 371-384.
Cameron, J. and Werksman, J. (1991), *The Precautionary Principle: A Policy for Action in the Face of Uncertainty*, Centre for International Environmental Law, CIE background papers on international environmental law No.1, King's College, London.
Chichilnisky, Graciela, 1991, *Global environment and North-South Trade*, Stanford Institute for Theoretical Economics, Stanford, California, Technical Report No.31.
Chisholm, A.H. (1988), 'Sustainable Resource Use and Development: Uncertainty, Irreversibility and Rational Choice', In Tisdell, C. and Maitra, P. (eds), *Technological Change, Development and the Environment: Socio-Economic Perspectives*, pp.188-216.
Clarke, H.R. (1991), *Risk, Uncertainty and Irreversibility: Implications for Sustainable Development*, Discussion Paper No.13, Department of Economics, La Trobe University.
Cline, W.R. (1991), 'Scientific Basis for the Greenhouse Effect', *The Economic Journal*, 101, pp.904-909.
CMIE, (1989) *Market and Market Shares*, Center for Monitoring Indian Economy, Bombay, November.
Coase, R.H. (1988) *The Firm, the Market and the Law*, The University of Chicago Press, Chicago/London.
Coase, R. H. (1960). 'The Problem of Social Cost', *Journal of Law and Economics*, 3, pp.1-44; reprinted in Coase, R.H. (1988), *The Firm, the Market and the Law*, University of Chicago Press, Chicago.
Coase, R.H. (1974) 'The lighthouse in economics', *The Journal of Law and Economics* 17, No. 2, pp.357-76.
Constantinescu, Vlad (1991a), 'La subsidiarité comme principe constitutionnel de l'intégration européenne', *Außenwirtschaft*, No.46, p.439-459.
Constantinescu, Vlad (1991b), 'Subsidiarität: Magisches Wort oder Handlungsprinzip der Europäischen Union', *Zeitschrift für Europäisches Wirtschaftsrecht*, p.561-563.
Dasgupta, P. (1982), *The Control of Resources*, Basil Blackwell, Oxford.
Dasgupta P.S. and G. M. Heal (1979), *Economic Theory and Exhaustible Resources*. Cambridge University Press, Cambridge
Dourojeanni, Marc J. (1989), 'The Environmental Impact of Cocoa Cultivation and Cocaine Production in the Peruvian Amazon Basin'.
ECLAC (1991), *Inventario y Cuentas del Patrimonio Natural en América Latina y el Caribe*, Santiago.
Eiselstein, Claus (1991), 'Europäische Verfassungsgebung. Einige grundsätzliche Überlegungen im Vorfeld der Regierungskonferenz', *Zeitschrift für Rechtspolitik*, pp.18-24.
Elazar, Daniel J. (1987), *Exploring Federalism*, University of Alabama Press, Tuscaloosca, Alabama.
Farber, S. (1991), 'Regulatory Schemes and Self-Protective Environmental Risk Control: A Comparison of Insurance, Liability, and Deposit/Refund Systems', *Ecological Economics*, 3, pp.231-245.
Filgueiras Cavalcante, Ophir (1991), 'A questao ambientale e o Direito Brasileiro', in Dourado, Maria Cristina (ed.), *Direito Ambiental e a Questao Amazonica*, Asociaçao de Universidades Amazonicas, Brazil.
Fisher, A.C. and Hanemann, W.M. (1986), *Information and the Dynamics of Environmental Protection: The Concept of the Critical Period*, Working Paper No.420, Division of Agriculture and Natural Resources, University of California.
Fisher, A.C. and Hanemann, W.M. (1990), 'Option Value: theory and measurement', *European Review of Agricultural Economics*, 17, pp.167-180.
Flavin, Ch., 1989, *Slowing Global Warming: A Worldwide Strategy*. Worldwatch Paper No.91, Washington, D.C.
Flory, Luis J. (1989), 'La prevención de la contaminación hídrica y la gestión de la Empresa Obras Sanitarias de la Nación (Argentina)', *Ambiente y Recursos Naturales*, vol.IV, No.4, Oct.-Dec. Buenos Aires.
Frenkel, Max (1984), *Föderalismus und Bundesstaat*, Lang, Bern, vol.1.
Frenkel, Max (1986), *Föderalismus und Bundesstaat*, Lang, Bern, vol.2.
Fritsch, Bruno, 1990, *Mensch, Umwelt, Wissen: evolutionsgeschichtliche Aspekte des Umweltproblems*, Verl.d. Fachvereine, Teubner, Zürich, Stuggart.
Fundación Natura, 'Institucionalización de las Actividades de la Conservación y la legislación en el Ecuador', in Dourado, Maria Cristina (ed.), *Direito Ambiental e a Questao Amazonica*, Asociaça de Universidades Amazonicas, Brazil.
GATT (1992) *International Trade 1990-1991*, Vol.1, chap. 3.

Grabitz, Eberhard, 'Article 130r', in E. Grabitz (ed.), *EWG-Vertrag, Kommentar* (loose-leaf), C.H. Beck, Munich.
Gündling, Lothar (1988), 'Umweltschutz in einer übernationalen Wirtschaftsgemeinschaft', in Weber B. and L. Gündling (eds.), *Dicke Luft in Europa - Aufgaben und Probleme der europäischen Umweltpolitik*, p.21-40, C.F. Muller, Heidelberg.
Hafner, Gerhard (1991), 'Liability and Compensation', *Yearbook of International Environmental Law*, vol. 2, p.91-98.
Heal, G. M. (1989) 'Economy and Climate: A Preliminary Framework for Microeconomic Analysis', in Just, R.E. & N. Bockstael (eds), *Commodity and Resource Policies in Agricultural Systems*, Springer, Berlin, Heidelberg, New York.
Heal, G. M. (1991). 'Risk Management and the Greenhouse Effect'. Presented at the First Nordic Conference on the Greenhouse Effect in Copenhagen, September, 1991. To be published in the proceedings under the editorship of Bert Bolin and Steve Schneider.
Hitzler, Gerhard (1991), 'Subsidiarität: Die Kommission gibt sich Mühe', *EG Magazin*, No. 5, p.13-15.
Hochbaum, Ingo (1992), 'Kohäsion und Subsidiarität - Maastricht und die Länderhoheit', *Die Öffentliche Verwaltung*, p.285-292.
Hohmann, Harald (1992), *Präventive Rechtspflichten und -prinzipien des modernen Umweltvölkerrechts*, Duncker & Humblot, Berlin.
IDB (1983), *Economic and Social Progress Report for Latin America*, Washington D.C.
IDB (1991), *Economic and Social Progress Report for Latin America*, Washington, D.C.
Joeres, Erhard F. and Martin H. David, (eds.), 1983, *Buying a Better Environment: Cost-Effective Regulation through Permit Trading*, Land Economics Monographs, No. 6, Madison/Wisc.
Keynes, John Maynard (1936) *The general theory of employment, interest and money*, Macmillan, London.
Knight, F.H., (1921) *Risk, uncertainty and profit*, New York.
Koo, Anthony, Y.C, Maureen Kallick, James Morgan and Soo-Yong Kim (1979), *Environmental Repercussions of Trade and Investment*, Michigan State University, East Lansing, Michigan.
Krämer, Ludwig (1991), 'Article 130r', in Groeben/Thiesing/Ehlermann, *Kommentar zum EWG-Vertrag*, 4 edn. Nomos, Baden-Baden.
Leme Machado, Alfonso (1989), 'Direito Ambiental Brasileiro', *Revista Dos Tribunais*, Sao Paulo.
Leonard, H. Jeffrey and Christopher J. Duerksen (1980), 'Environmental Regulation and the Location of Industry: an international perspective'. *The Columbia Journal of World Business* (Summer).
Leopold, Aldo (1949) *A sand county almanac*, Oxford University Press, New York.
Lipton, M. (1983) *Poverty, undernutrition and hunger*, World Bank Staff Working Paper No.597, Washington D.C.
Loomes, G. and Sugden, R. (1982), 'Regret Theory: An Alternative Theory of Rational Choice Under Uncertainty', *Economic Journal*, 92, pp.805-24.
Marcic, René (1957), *Vom Gesetzesstaat zum Rechtsstaat*, Wien.
McDonald, S.L. (1971). *Petroleum Conservation in the United States: an Economic Analysis*. Johns Hopkins Press, Baltimore.
Menell, P.S. (1991), 'The Limitations of Legal Institutions for Addressing Environmental Risks', *The Journal of Economic Perspectives*, 5:3, pp.93-113.
Mohr, E. (1991), 'Global Warming: Economic Policy in the Face of Positive and Negative Spillovers', in Siebert, H. and T. Mohr, (eds) *Environmental Scarcity: The International Dimension*, University of Michigan press, pp.213-215.
Nordhaus, W.D. (1990), 'Economic Approaches to Greenhouse Warming', Paper prepared for a Conference: Economic Policy Responses to Global Warming, Palazzo Colonna, Rome.
NSSO (1990) 'Results of the NSS 37th Round (1982)', *Sarvekshana*, Vol XIII No.3 Issue No.42, Jan-March.
OECD (1972) *Guiding Principles Concerning the International Economic Aspects of Environmental Policies*, Paris.
OECD (1975) *The Polluter Pays Principle: Definition, Analysis, Implementation*, Paris.
OECD (1985) Communiqué, Environment Ministers Meeting at Ministerial Level, Declaration on Environment Resources for the Future, Paris.
OECD (1986) *OECD and the Environment*, 1986 and update, Paris.
OECD (1986b) *The Guidelines for Multinational Enterprises*, Paris.
OECD (1987a) *Pricing of Water Services*, Paris.
OECD (1987b) *Recommendation on Water Resource Management Policies: Integration, Demand Management and Groundwater Protection*, Paris.

OECD (1989) *Economic Instruments for Environmental Protection*, Paris.

OECD (1990) *Valuation of Environmental Benefits*, Paris.

OECD (1991a) Communiqué, Environment Committee Meeting at Ministerial Level. An Environment Strategy in the 1990s. SG/PRESS (91)9, Paris, 31st January 1991.

OECD (1991b) *Environmental policy: how to apply economic instruments*, Paris.

OECD (1991c) *Recommendation of the Council on the Use of Economic Instruments in Environmental Policy*, Paris.

OECD (1991d) *Resource Pricing*, Background Paper n°2, OECD Environment Committee Meeting at Ministerial Level, Paris.

OECD (1991e) *State of the Environment*, Paris.

OECD (1992a) *Convention on Climate Change: Economic Aspects of Negotiation*, Paris

OECD (1992b) *The Polluter-Pays Principle: OECD analyses and recommendations*, Paris.

Opschoor, J.B. (1991) 'Economic Instruments for Controlling Persistent Micropollutants', pp.163-176, in: Opschoor, J.B. and Pearce, D.W. (eds.), *Persistent Pollutants*, Kluwer, Dordrecht/Boston/London.

Ortuzar, Antonio (1992), 'Environmental Protection', mimeo, in 'Conference on Legal Aspects of Foreign Investment in Latin America: the case of Chile', American University, Washington, D.C. 16 January.

Ossenbühl, Fritz (1990), (ed.), *Föderalismus und Regionalismus in Europa*, Nomos, Baden-Baden.

Pearce, D. (1991), 'The Role of Carbon Taxes in Adjusting to Global Warming', *The Economic Journal*, 101, pp.938-948.

Pearce, David (1989) 'Economic incentives and renewable natural resource management', in OECD, *Renewable natural resources*, Paris.

Pezzey, John (1988) 'Market Mechanisms of Pollution Control: 'Polluter Pays', Economic and Practical Aspects'', in Turner, R. Kerry (ed) *Sustainable Environment Management*, Belhaven press, London.

Plato, 'The Dialogues of Plato', vol. 4 'The Laws', book 8, section 485(e), Translator B. Jowett, Clarendon Press, Oxford, 4 edn., 1953.

Quiggin, J. (1982), 'A Theory of Anticipated Utility', *Journal of Economic Behaviour and Organisation*, 3, pp.323-43.

Quiggin, J. and J. Horowitz, (1992), *Estimating the Costs of Global Warming: Comparative Static and Dynamic Approaches*, mimeo, Department of Agricultural and Resource Economics, University of Maryland.

Rauschining, Dietrich (1981), Lac Lanoux Arbitration, in Bernhardt, Rudolf (ed.), *Encyclopedia of Public International Law*, vol. 2, p.166-168, North Holland, Amsterdam.

Ready, R.C. and R.C. Bishop, (1991), 'Endangered Species and the Safe Minimum Standard', *American Journal of Agricultural Economics*, 73:2, pp.309-312.

Repetto, Robert *et al.* (1991a), *Accounts Overdue: Natural Resource Depletion in Costa Rica*, WRI, Washington, D.C.

Repetto, Robert *et al.* (1991b), . *Wasting assets: natural resources in the national income accounts*, WRI, Washington, D.C.

Rose, Roger (1992) 'Valuing environmental services', in Wallace, Nancy, *Natural Resource Management: an Economic Perspective*, Australian Bureau of Agricultural Resource Economics, Canberra.

Schaefer-Guignier, Otto (1990) 'De l'émancipation des animaux au droit de la nature', *Cahiers du christianisme social*, Spring.

Schelling, Thomas C, (1992), 'Some Economics of Global Warming,' *American Economic Review*, 82:1, March, pp.1-14.

Schelling, T.C. (1990), 'International Burden Sharing and Coordination: Prospects for Cooperative Approaches to Global Warming,' Paper prepared for a Conference: Economic Policy Responses to Global Warming, Palazzo Colonna, Rome.

Schmidhuber, Peter M. and Gerhard Hitzler (1992), 'Die Verankerung des Subsidiaritätsprinzip im EWG-Vertrag - ein wichtiger Schritt auf dem Weg zu einer föderalen Verfassung der Europäischen Gemeinschaft', *Neue Zeitschrift für Verwaltungsrecht* p.720-725.

Siebert, Horst (1987) *Economics of the environment*, Springer-Verlag, second edition, Berlin.

Tietenberg, Thomas H., (1980) 'Transferable Discharge Permits and the Control of Stationary Source Air Pollution: A Survey and Synthesis,' *Land Economics*, 56, pp.391-416.

Tietenberg, Thomas, H., (1985) *Emissions Trading*, Washington, D.C.; Resources for the Future.

Tobey, James (1990) 'The Effects of Domestic Environmental Policies on Patterns of World Trade: An Empirical Test', *Kyklos*, Vol. 43.

Turner, R. Kerry (1991) 'Economics and wetland management', *Ambio*, Vol. 20, No. 2, April.

UNCED (1992a), 'Agenda 21', A/CONF.151/4 (Part IV).

UNCED (1992b), Preparatory Committee document A/CONF.151/PC/101, 23 January.

UNCTAD (1990) *Sustainable development and UNCTAD activities*, TD/B/1267.

UNCTAD (1991) *Policies and mechanisms for achieving sustainable development*, TD/B/1304.

UNCTAD (1992) *Combating global warming: study on a global system of tradeable carbon emission entitlements*, UNCTAD/RDP/DFP/1.

UNCTC (1988), 'Transnational Corporation in World Development: Trends and Prospects', E,88,II.A.7.

UNEP (1984), 'The State of the Environment 1984: the environment in the dialogue between and among developed and developing countries'(GC 12/11), Nairobi.

United Nations Statistical Office (1990), COMTRADE database.

Walbeck, M. and J. Wagner, (1987) *Anhaltszahlen für die CO_2-Emission durch die Energieversorgung. Systemforschung und technologische Entwicklung*. Jülich.

Walter, I (1982) *Environmentally Induced Industrial Relocation to Developing Countries, Environment and Trade*.

Weitzman, M. L. (1974). 'Prices vs Quantities'. *Review of Economic Studies*, XLI (4), pp.477-91.

Whalley, J. and R. Wigle, (1990), 'The International Incidence of Carbon Taxes', Paper prepared for a Conference: Economic Policy Responses to Global Warming, Palazzo Colonna, Rome.

World Bank (1992) *Development and the Environment, World Development Report 1992*, Oxford University Press, Oxford.

World Bank (1991) *The Challenge of Development, World Development report, 1991*, Oxford University Press, Oxford.

World Commission on Environment and Development (1987) *Our Common Future*, Oxford University Press, Oxford.

INDEX